About Island Press

Since 1984, the nonprofit Island Press has been stimulating, shaping, and communicating the ideas that are essential for solving environmental problems worldwide. With more than 800 titles in print and some 40 new releases each year, we are the nation's leading publisher on environmental issues. We identify innovative thinkers and emerging trends in the environmental field. We work with world-renowned experts and authors to develop cross-disciplinary solutions to environmental challenges.

Island Press designs and implements coordinated book publication campaigns in order to communicate our critical messages in print, in person, and online using the latest technologies, programs, and the media. Our goal: to reach targeted audiences—scientists, policymakers, environmental advocates, the media, and concerned citizens—who can and will take action to protect the plants and animals that enrich our world, the ecosystems we need to survive, the water we drink, and the air we breathe.

Island Press gratefully acknowledges the support of its work by the Agua Fund, Inc., Annenberg Foundation, The Christensen Fund, The Nathan Cummings Foundation, The Geraldine R. Dodge Foundation, Doris Duke Charitable Foundation, The Educational Foundation of America, Betsy and Jesse Fink Foundation, The William and Flora Hewlett Foundation, The Kendeda Fund, The Andrew W. Mellon Foundation, The Curtis and Edith Munson Foundation, Oak Foundation, The Overbrook Foundation, the David and Lucile Packard Foundation, The Summit Fund of Washington, Trust for Architectural Easements, Wallace Global Fund, The Winslow Foundation, and other generous donors.

The opinions expressed in this book are those of the author(s) and do not necessarily reflect the views of our donors.

DESIGN WITH MICROCLIMATE

ROBERT D. BROWN

DESIGN WITH MICROCLIMATE

The Secret to Comfortable Outdoor Space

ISLANDPRESS

Washington | Covelo | London

ISLAND PRESS is a trademark of the Center for Resource Economics.

Library of Congress Cataloging-in-Publication Data

Brown, Robert D.
Design with microclimate : the secret to comfortable outdoor space / Robert Brown.
p.   cm.
Includes bibliographical references and index.
ISBN-13: 978-1-59726-739-7 (cloth : alk. paper)
ISBN-10: 1-59726-739-2 (cloth : alk. paper)
ISBN-13: 978-1-59726-740-3 (pbk. : alk. paper)
ISBN-10: 1-59726-740-6 (pbk. : alk. paper) 1. Landscape architecture—Climatic
factors.· I. Title.
⌐ SB475.9.C55B75   2010
  712—dc22

                                        2010008331

Printed using Berkeley and Avant Garde

Printed on recycled, acid-free paper

Manufactured in the United States of America
10 9 8 7 6 5 4 3 2 1

KEYWORDS: Solar radiation, terrestrial radiation, air temperature and humidity,
natural heating and cooling, energy budget, thermal comfort, energy-efficient design,
water-efficient design, site assessment, microclimate adjustment

For Karen, my wonderful daughter

CONTENTS

ACKNOWLEDGMENTS

Thanks to Jeffrey Brown for drawing many of the figures in the book. Heather Boyer, my editor, and Courtney Lix, my editorial assistant, were absolutely terrific. They made the process smooth and enjoyable, and this book is much better as a result of their input.

1
EXPERIENTIAL

We've gotten pretty used to being thermally comfortable. Temperatures of our indoor environments are so well regulated that we are cozy warm on the coldest winter days and pleasantly cool on the hottest summer days. In contrast, though, many of our *outdoor* environments are not thermally comfortable. We have to lean into bitterly cold winter winds as we slog through slush to get from our car to the store. We have to endure withering heat as we try to find a place to eat our lunch outside on beautiful, sunny summer days. But it doesn't have to be that way. Outdoor environments can be designed to be thermally comfortable in almost any weather conditions and at almost any time of the day or year. This book will help you learn how to do it.

People love to spend time outside—strolling, interacting with nature, gossiping with friends, visiting shops, lingering over a cappuccino in an outdoor café. Landscape architects and urban designers strive to design places that encourage these kinds of activities, places where people will want to spend their time. However, their designs often focus on such elements as physical attractiveness, functionality, and composition. These are all important, of course, but without one invisible, intriguing component of the landscape they are doomed to failure. Unless people are thermally comfortable in the space, they simply won't use it. Although few people are even aware of the effects that design can have on the sun, wind, humidity, and air temperature in a space, a thermally comfortable microclimate is the very foundation of well-loved and well-used outdoor places.

When we are fortunate enough to see something through new eyes, it can be a powerful learning experience. It can provide sudden insight and depth of understanding that can change our lives forever. I hope that this book will change your perspective on the value of considering micro-climate in designing outdoor spaces. I have found that people have a per-spective on microclimate that they have gained through many years of living with and experiencing it. Yet this experiential understanding is usu-ally far from complete—and, often, is completely wrong.

Let's take an everyday situation of walking toward a tall building with a moderate to strong wind at your back. As you near the building, you notice that the wind seems to shift directions and is now coming *out* of the building toward you. Have you every wondered how that could be? Well, here is what is happening. In general, the wind increases in speed the higher you go above the ground, so the wind that encounters the front of the building near the top is traveling faster than the wind at ground level. When it reaches the building, it has to go somewhere—some of it goes up and over the building, some around the sides, and some down the face, all the while maintaining much of its speed. When the wind that flows down the front reaches the ground, it again has to go somewhere, and much of it ends up flowing *away* from the face of the building. It's as if it is rebounding from the building, and you experience it as if it is flowing *out* of the building. So the next time you see images of people struggling against the wind to get into a building, picture the mechanism that has caused that to happen. You will never think of the wind around a building in the same way again. And that's really the intent of this book: to help you see and understand microclimates, maybe not so that your eyes can see them but so that your mind can.

We are all experiencing microclimates at all times—it's almost like walking around in your own personal microclimatic bubble—but most of us are totally unaware of it and don't understand or appreciate its im-portance. Much of the microclimate is totally invisible to us—unless it is brought to our attention in a way that we can visualize, we don't even know that it's there—but nevertheless it can play a very important role in our lives.

When I was a kid, I spent a lot of time at my grandparents' farm in Saskatchewan, Canada. I remember the winters the most. A cold wind was always blowing from the west. When my brothers and I would be shooed outside to play, we knew that when we got cold we could go around to the south side of the house and squat down beside the lone spruce tree in the yard. There was hardly any wind there, and the sun felt like warm hands on our frozen cheeks and noses. I never questioned why it would be so much warmer there than anywhere else in the landscape. That's just the way it was.

People have been seeking warm places on cold days for a very long time. Evidence points to a time about forty thousand years ago when some people decided to wander out of Africa and start to live in less-than-warm-all-the-time climates, and ever since we've tried to figure out ways to stay warm on cool days.

Those people who stayed in Africa didn't have to spend much time try-ing to stay warm. The climate throughout most of Africa was, and still is, generally pretty comfortable for people. It's tropical, subtropical, desert, or savannah, and where there's more than one season it is usually a wet season and a dry season. Much of Africa hasn't seen a frost in living memory. In fact, the people who live there spend much more time trying to keep from getting too hot than they ever do trying to keep from getting cold.

A few years ago, I was working on a research project in the remote vil-lages of Malawi, a tiny country in southern Africa. My Malawian research partners and I would converse with local communities about the way they use their land and how we might be able to help them achieve some of their goals.

I found it interesting to see where we would hold our community meeting. It was always selected by the village headman, it was always outside, and it was always a place that was pleasantly cool. In one village, it was in the shade of the bicycle repair shop (see figure 1.1). Even on the

Figure 1.1 The community meeting place in this small village in Malawi was on the porch of the bicycle repair shop. There was just enough room for everyone to sit in the shade.

hottest days that I experienced in Africa, these community meeting places were always comfortably cool.

The villages we visited didn't have electricity, so it goes without saying that they didn't have air-conditioning available to cool them off on hot days. They have to use whatever is at hand, and they have learned through trial and error over a very long time what works and what doesn't. Traditional methods of building homes and communities provided a lot of shade and allowed a lot of air to flow around and through buildings. One day I talked with some local fellows who were building a home in a fishing village near Lake Chilwa—dozens of kilometers from the nearest electrical outlet. This wasn't exactly your typical beach-front property. The boats that the local fishers used were dugout canoes—quite literally, big trees that had been felled and had their insides carved out.

The homes were small, round huts made from stacks of sun-dried mud bricks, topped with a thatched roof. I was curious why they left a space between the top of the wall and the roof. The builders didn't know. They said that it was just the way houses were built in that area. It was just standard practice. When I asked if maybe the space was there to allow air to move through the hut on hot nights, they perked up and agreed that yes, in fact, the huts were quite cool at night. They had never really thought about it before, they said, but now that I mentioned it, there was often a bit of a cool breeze on hot nights. It seemed that the reason for the building form had been lost in time but that the effect of building that way continued to benefit the inhabitants.

It seems that our ancestors who decided to stay in Africa have learned to live in a hot climate and stay reasonably comfortable. But what about the ones who emigrated into regions that were not warm year-round? What about our ancestors who wandered north into Asia, Europe, and the Americas? People began to live in areas that had a distinctly cold season for part of each year. How did they stay warm?

Part of the answer, of course, is that they developed warm clothing. Animal furs can be very effective at keeping the cold out, as can many other natural fibers and materials. But warm clothing wasn't enough. People had to find locations to live that would not require them to spend too much time or energy trying to stay warm. One of the most popular early homes seems to have been caves—especially those that open toward the sun.[1] People would have noticed that during hot summer days it was comfortably cool in the cave, and that during cold weather they were much warmer in the cave than they were outside. Part of this was due to the thick walls of the cave, which buffered the thermal effects of changing seasons, like good insulation in the walls of a house. But part of it was also because during the winter the sun was low in the sky and could penetrate deep into the cave—warming everything that it hit—while in the summer the high sun angle meant that the interior of the cave was shady all day.

Besides cool air temperatures, our ancestors about two thousand generations ago would have also had to deal with wind on cold days.[2] The cooling effect of wind on people increases as wind speed increases and also as air temperature goes down. So people had to find a way to get out of the wind during the winter. The cave helped here as well. Wind doesn't blow into a cave very well, especially if the cave is a dead end. Any air that tries to enter the cave has nowhere to go and is effectively blocked by back pressure. The advantage of south-facing caves is that winter winds seldom blow from the south—and if they do, they aren't very cold. Cold winter winds in the northern hemisphere often blow from westerly and northerly directions, so they are effectively blocked by the walls of south-facing caves.

Through trial and error over long periods of time, people learned to create thermally comfortable environments in a wide range of climatic conditions. Although this can be a very effective technique, it takes a long time and often requires many failures along the way. We are now much more strategic in our approaches, and we use the power of electronic computing and a solid understanding of energy flow to determine the effects of design ideas on the microclimate and thermal comfort of spaces *before* the ideas are implemented.

The foundation of design for thermal comfort is the *energy budget of a person*. It's not unlike the budget that a student would have when attending university. A student typically would have a certain amount of money to spend each year, and if more goes to tuition, then there is less available for other things. In the same way, a human body has inputs and outputs of energy, and there has to be a balance between the two or the body will become overheated or underheated. These models assume that a person's core temperature has to stay within a narrow range or the person will begin to feel uncomfortable. Keeping a human body thermally comfortable in changing seasons is no mean feat. Your internal body temperature can range from only about 36°C to 38°C (roughly 97°F to 100°F); if it goes lower than that, you are risking hypothermia, and going higher than that could bring on hyperthermia—and death! That's a remarkably narrow range, especially considering how much air temperature can change throughout the year. I've huddled against −50°C (−58°F) winds in northern Manitoba and perspired through +50°C (122°F) temperatures in Death Valley, California. And all that time I was maintaining an internal body temperature of 37°C (98.6°F) plus or minus one degree. Amazing!

The first study to look in detail at the internal temperatures of people was done in Germany. It reported that the average temperature of human cores is 37°C. The study was translated into English, and the temperature was converted to Fahrenheit, resulting in the well-known value of 98.6°F as the *normal* temperature. Lost in translation was that the original study calculated an average of all the temperatures measured and then *rounded* the answer off to the nearest degree Celsius. A mathematically valid conversion would round off the answer to the nearest Fahrenheit degree as well. The number after the decimal (the .6) gave the impression of a value that was known to the nearest tenth of a degree, while in fact it was recorded and reported to only the nearest degree. Now that more careful measurements have been taken with more precise and accurate instruments, it is well accepted that the average normal internal temperature of a person is 98.2°F plus or minus 0.6°F. Anything within the range of 97.6° to 98.8°F is completely normal. So the value that everyone knows—that our normal temperature is 98.6°F—is wrong. It is the remnant of a poorly translated scientific study.

This average normal internal temperature of a person is the important starting point of energy budget modeling. From this point we consider flows of energy to and from the body. The human body really has only two main sources of energy or *heat* available to it. The first source of heat is that generated inside the body through metabolism. The more work you do, the more heat you generate. When I do my sloth imitation in front of the television on Sunday afternoon, I'm not generating much metabolic energy—probably about 60 watts for every square meter of surface area of my body (W/m^2). Even if I really speed up my arm as it moves those chips toward my mouth, or if I move my thumb super fast on the remote control, I'm not going to generate more than a few more watts. Contrast that to the rare times I get out and toss around a football for half an hour. Before I've chased down many bad throws, I'll be generating upward of 250 W/m^2 and will find myself taking off layers of clothing to cool down.

The other main source of energy available to our bodies is radiation. Now, for those of us who grew up with parents warning us of the dangers of radiation—from microwave ovens to nuclear power plants—the idea of using radiation to warm ourselves can be frightening. But this is a different kind of radiation, one you experience all the time. The largest amount of radiation available to heat our bodies comes from the sun and is known as solar radiation. It's more than just sunlight, though; a good portion of it— about half—is invisible to the human eye. It's there but we can't see it. If that isn't weird enough, the other source of radiant energy is being emitted by everything around us. This book, the walls, everything surrounding us, is emitting radiation all the time, and it's also invisible to the human eye. *There's invisible radiant energy all around us, Scotty.* It sounds like a script for a sci-fi movie.

I'll spare you the details of radiation for now, but let me just say that after all these years of living with radiation, and studying it in almost every way possible, we still don't really know what it is or how it works. Or maybe I should say, we have lots of ways of understanding and describing it, but these ways depend on how we are looking at it. In some ways, radiation acts like a wave, much like those in the ocean. It has peaks and valleys, and the distance between peaks determines the wavelength. When we see different colors, we are seeing different wavelengths of light. Blue light has a shorter wavelength (the peaks of the waves are closer together) than red light. When the wavelengths get much shorter than blue or much longer than red, our eyes can no longer see them. But they're still there.

In other ways, radiation acts like little parcels of energy called photons. When plants photosynthesize solar radiation, it can be understood as taking little bundles of energy from the sunlight and using it to make plant material.

But for now, let's just think of radiation as an input into a person's energy budget. And it can be a very big input. If you stand outside on a sunny day, you could be getting upward of one thousand watts per square meter of solar energy striking your body—more than ten times the amount I was generating while lying on the couch.

In terms of inputs of energy to our bodies, that's about it—unless you are wearing electric socks or sitting in a sauna. If you're a bit chilly and want to add energy to your body, you can either generate more internal energy by working harder or move your body into the sun or near a warm surface, such as a fire or a radiator.

Now, if you've been paying attention, you might say, *Hey, wait a minute. . . . I can warm up by putting on more clothes!* While it's true that this would make you feel warmer, you wouldn't actually be adding any heat to your body. You would simply be slowing down the loss of heat from your body.

As you might expect, the ways that a human body can lose heat are as simple as the ways that it can gain heat. There are four main ways: through convection, evaporation, conduction, and—there it is again—radiation.

Convection is what happens when air moves past your body and carries away energy. As long as the air is cooler than your approximately 33°C (91°F) skin temperature, then as the air molecules collide with your skin they grab some energy and take it with them. This warms the air molecules ever so slightly and cools your skin a wee bit. Let a few billion air molecules strike your skin, however, and you will start to sit up and take notice.

The more air molecules that strike your skin, the more energy that will be carried away, which means that the faster the air is moving the more convection that will take place and the cooler you will feel. The amount of cooling that takes place also depends on the temperature difference between your skin and the air. If the air is the same temperature as your skin, then no exchange of energy will take place and there will be no convective cooling. However, when the air molecules are much colder than your skin, substantial cooling can occur.

The second way a body can shed energy is through evaporation. The most obvious, but by no means the only, way to understand this is to think about a hot day when you sweated so much that your underarms got wet. OK, maybe that's not an image you want to have—so let's imagine instead that you have a buff body and that you were exercising so hard that perspiration formed on your chest. In either case, the liquid water that oozes out of your pores and onto your skin might have an opportunity to evaporate by changing state into its gaseous form. If this happens, and it often does as long as the humidity in the air is not too high, then it takes a lot of energy with it. The loss of this energy from your body makes you feel cooler.

The third main way to lose energy from your body is through conduction. In this case, energy passes directly from your body to another object that is in contact with your body. The image that always comes to my mind when I think of conduction is one from my childhood. When I would stay over at my grandparents' place, I used to wear only light pajama bottoms to bed and in the morning couldn't afford the time it took to put on more clothes in my rush to get the best seat for breakfast (best meaning closer than my brothers to the pancake stack). The chairs in the kitchen were typical 1950s-style chairs made of enameled steel. There was no gentle, comfortable way to settle into one of those chairs—I simply had to plop down and let the heat drain from my body into the chair. It was as bracing as diving into a cold northern lake in the springtime. I didn't know it at the time, but it was conduction that was drawing the heat from my nearly naked body and using it to warm the chair. The molecules in my skin were transferring some of their energy to the molecules in the chair, and I experienced it as a feeling of coldness.

The final main way that your body loses energy is through radiation. I mentioned earlier that everything is emitting radiation, and I wasn't kidding. Even you! The molecules that you are made up of (more than half of which are water molecules) vibrate based on their temperature and generate waves of radiant energy. The warmer you are, the faster your molecules vibrate and the more energy you emit. This is one of your body's very effective ways to keep from getting overheated and allowing your core to go beyond that critical 38°C (100°F) threshold. While your core temperature needs to stay a constant temperature, your skin can get quite a bit cooler or warmer than that and thereby regulate how much terrestrial radiation you emit.

Now, the really interesting thing about all this heat gain and heat loss is, as I said earlier, that the gain and loss *have to balance*. The amount of heat that is added to your body has to exactly match the amount of heat that is lost. If it doesn't, then the internal temperature of your body will go above or below the small window of acceptable core temperatures of 36° to 38°C (97° to 100°F) and you will become hypothermic or hyperthermic.

So, let's have a quick review. People can control the amount of heat coming into their bodies by changing their activity level or by modifying the amount of radiation they receive. They can control the amount of heat being lost from their bodies by opening or restricting the heat loss channels of conduction, convection, evaporation, and radiation. It sounds complicated, but we have all learned to deal with it simply and effectively all day, every day, without even thinking about it. If you are walking along a street and start to feel too warm, you might decide to take off your jacket (reduce the insulation around your body and allow more convective cooling) or cross over to the shady side of the street (reduce the input of solar radiation). Or, if you're standing in a plaza and start to feel chilly, you might sidle over into the sun (increase the input of solar radiation) or put on a sweater (increase insulation value).

People unconsciously modify the various streams of energy into and away from their bodies all the time. Our bodies naturally seek a balance of energy, and if the balance starts to tip one way or the other, we will try to move it back toward the equilibrium point. As long as the outdoor space has a microclimate that is not extremely hot or cold, people have several strategies available to help make their own personal microclimate comfortable, or at least tolerable. The strategies that people have for making themselves warmer or cooler in an outdoor environment generally fall into three categories: (1) we can put on and take off articles of clothing, (2) we can increase or decrease our activity level, and (3) we can move our bodies.

Besides these main categories, a wide variety of novelty comfort devices that defy categorization are available commercially. These include the handheld mini-fan that will increase convective heat loss, hand warmers that heat the inside of your pocket, and electric socks that run on batteries strapped to your calf. Many of these devices can be very effective for strategic heating or cooling in extreme environments. In fact, my buddies and I won the unofficial endurance competition at a football game one time using a novelty personal heating device. Allow me to diverge for a minute to make a point.

One year my friends and I went to watch a championship football game in Saskatoon, Saskatchewan, where the air temperature at game time was −40°C (−40°F). Minus forty! We wore lots of well-insulated clothing and covered as much exposed skin as possible (to reduce our convective cooling). Only our faces were uncovered. We took well-insulated pads to sit on (to reduce the conductive heat loss into the concrete seats). We carried insulated flasks so we could occasionally inject hot liquid into our body core (our substitute for generating internal energy). And we put hand warmers into our pockets so when our fingers approached frostbite levels they could be briefly resurrected.

Of course, attending a game under such conditions is only partly about the game on the field. The real game is in the stands. It can be described as the *let's-see-who-can-stay-outside-the-longest-without-having-to-go-in-to-warm-up* game. We had a secret weapon, a catalytic heater that emits large amounts of radiation, and the competition didn't stand a chance. We huddled around the device, which was carefully concealed at our feet, and by halftime we had blown the competition away. The few fans left in the stands were making increasingly frequent trips into the warm underbelly of the stadium to warm up, while the three of us hadn't moved. The wavelength of the radiation from the heater was longer than that of solar radiation, but the feeling that we got when it was absorbed by our fingers was no different than if we were basking on a beach in Bermuda.

Now, the point of this story is not that you can build any kind of outdoor environment that you want and a few hardy (maybe foolhardy) people will manage to find a way to use it. The point really is that if you aren't careful in designing places, you'll create microclimates that are beyond the potential of being comfortable for the majority of people. A *slightly* uncomfortable microclimate can be tolerated by a person who is willing to add or remove clothing, increase activity level, or move a little to find a more comfortable microclimate. However, if the microclimate is outside this *range of tolerance*, then personal strategies cannot make it comfortable. One responsibility of a landscape architect—arguably one of the most important responsibilities—is to design environments that will create microclimates that are within people's range of tolerance so that people using the space will be thermally comfortable or will be close enough to being comfortable that they can use their personal strategies to make themselves comfortable.

The football game was spectacular, yet few people stayed in the stands to watch because they were simply too cold. This extreme example is played out in more subtle ways every day in countless outdoor spaces around the world. People would love to be outside eating their lunches, visiting with friends, people watching. But so many outdoor spaces are uncomfortably hot or cold and are outside the range of tolerance of personal strategies that few people use them.

So, how can outdoor places be designed so that they are thermally comfortable? One approach is to look at successful places from the past and see what forms and patterns have evolved and persisted. I have a hypothesis that only *microclimatically successful* places survive the test of time. If an outdoor space created thermally *uncomfortable* microclimates, few people would ever use it. Over time, it would have little opportunity to become an important place for people, and nobody would care very much if it was removed. On the other hand, if an outdoor space created positive microclimates, people would likely use it and it might become an important place for them. Any proposal to remove it would likely be protested by these people. I like to call this the *enduring microclimate hypothesis*. It basically says that landscapes that create positive microclimates are likely to endure, while negative microclimates are likely to be removed or replaced over time.

The meeting places in Malawian villages that I mentioned earlier are patterns that have persisted over a long period of time. We now understand that the shade reduces inputs of solar radiation, the breeze enhances convective and evaporative cooling, and the seats—often flat rocks—enhance conductive cooling. However, this pattern was undoubtedly derived through trial and error and shared from village to village.

A good microclimate can also be one that is energy efficient, or water efficient, or in some way makes a more positive environment. A hill where the most snow accumulates in the winter might become a prized toboggan run. A pond where the ice freezes smoothly, providing a great skating surface, would receive wails of protest from the local kids if it were proposed to be drained. People appreciate positive microclimates even if they don't know or use that term.

One of my graduate students, Diane, investigated the microclimates of ancient patterns in the landscape of Apulia in southern Italy. She found a strong and consistent relationship, and there were more than a few interesting examples. She visited ancient olive groves and talked with the local people, who told her that some of the trees were one thousand years old or more. She noticed that piled around the base of these old trees were white rocks about the size of a fist. When she asked the locals why the rocks were there, they had no explanation other than "that's what everyone does."

When Diane investigated the microclimate of these rock piles by considering the flows of energy in the system, she found something fascinating. The white rocks tend to reflect a lot of the solar radiation that they receive, so they remain cooler than the adjacent dark soil. The rocks also provide an insulating layer between the soil at the base of the tree and the atmosphere, thus keeping this area cooler than if the rocks weren't there. The cooler soil remains moister than soil that isn't protected by the rocks, and any water that does evaporate would have a difficult time making it through the convoluted channels around and between the rocks. In essence, the rocks were providing a very effective *mulch* at the base of the trees that kept the roots cool and moist in a hot, dry climate. Because of their white color, the rocks were more effective than an organic mulch, such as bark chips, would have been. The local residents didn't know why they were doing it, but they knew that it was effective.

Another pattern that Diane noticed, as have other people over time, was the use of outdoor spaces in cities such as Bari. The daily rhythm of the people is strongly related to the climatic patterns. It's very hot and sunny by midday—simply too hot to work. So people traditionally have taken a break in the afternoon to have a light nap or at least to rest in the shade. Then, in the evenings, people flock to the *piazzas* to spend hours sipping espresso, eating gelato, and walking slowly around the perimeter, arm in arm, visiting with friends. While the days are very hot (and the unshaded piazzas are unbearably hot), the evenings cool off quickly. Soon after the sun goes down, the air starts to cool considerably, and if you were standing in the middle of a field outside of the city, you would be uncomfortably cool before the evening was very old. During the hot day, however, the piazzas are absorbing prodigious amounts of solar radiation and storing it in the rock walls and floors (see figure 1.2). In the evening, these warm surfaces emit large amounts of their stored heat through longwave radiation emission, bathing the people in its warmth and creating a thermally comfortable microclimate.

Diane also noticed, though, that some piazzas were not visited in the evenings. She asked local residents why they were avoided. It seems that they used to be places to visit in the evening but now nobody uses them, but there is no real explanation why. To solve this puzzle, Diane observed the piazzas throughout the day and evening, analyzed their microclimates, and then hit upon the explanation. It was the cars. In Italy these days, cars are everywhere. Ancient Italian cities were built long before there were cars, and no space was set aside for parking. So where do they park? Everywhere! Even on sidewalks and in piazzas. The piazzas that were sitting there unused during the day because of the heat seemed like ideal places for parking cars. However, what Diane noticed was that the cars got very hot during the day while parked in the piazzas. When people returned to their cars in the late afternoon, they had to gingerly get into their frighteningly hot seats and turn on their air conditioners before driving away. And in driving away, they were basically transporting the heat that had been absorbed by their cars *out of the piazza*. This meant that the stone walls and floor of the piazza had been kept cooler during the day, having been shaded by the cars. Then, when evening rolled around and people started to gather in the piazza, they found that something was wrong. They probably couldn't identify it, but it was not as thermally comfortable as it used

Figure 1.2 Urban piazzas in Apulia are almost empty during hot middays. In this late-afternoon image, the solar radiation is reflecting off the white building and still streaming into the piazza. These places come to life in the cool evening when crowds of people gather and are warmed by the terrestrial radiation being emitted from the hot walls and pavement of the piazza.

to be. The radiant energy that used to stream from the walls and floor of the piazza was reduced. It was just another uncomfortable urban space, and the people moved on to a different, more comfortable place—a piazza where cars did not park during the day.

A couple of relatively recent human-induced changes to our climate need to be included in our discussion at this point: global climate change and urban heat islands. It's clear that we have benefited from a relatively long period of stable climate, but now it's also quite clear that human activities are starting to upset that stability and create a more volatile climate. Some areas are becoming warmer, some cooler, some wetter, some drier. It's a critical issue that will require a concerted effort to counteract, and it's important that each individual try to limit his or her contribution of carbon dioxide. In reality, though, the effect of an individual is like a drop of water in the ocean. Don't get me wrong—we should absolutely be doing what we can to reduce our contributions to carbon dioxide in the atmosphere—but our individual contributions are very small. However, as individuals, we can each have an enormous impact on mitigating the impacts of climate change if we use the information in this book to design environments that are environmentally appropriate and thermally comfortable. It's probably too late to stop at least some climate change on a global scale—however, we can definitely modify the microclimates of outdoor places, even in a hotter, drier climate, to be thermally comfortable for people.

The second issue is similar in effect but more localized in extent. Urban areas tend to be warmer and drier than their surrounding countryside and are well known as urban heat islands. Similarly to global climate change, there is relatively little that an individual can do to reduce the urban heat island effect, but *as a microclimatic designer*, each individual can have an enormous positive effect on the thermal comfort of urban areas in spite of the urban heat island

It will be interesting to see, over time, whether or not places with uncomfortable microclimates will survive, especially if the global climate gets warmer and urban heat islands intensify. For example, the Boston City Hall Plaza (see figure 1.3) is an open, windswept, shadeless space that creates

Figure 1.3 The Boston City Hall Plaza has broad expanses of hard surfaces with few or no trees or overhead structures. During summer, the solar radiation load is very high and people using the plaza would be uncomfortably hot much of the time. In winter, the cold winds blow unobstructed through the area, creating uncomfortably cold conditions.

extremely uncomfortable microclimates: hot and sunny in summer, cold and windy in winter. Yet it persists, at least for now. In the short term, there might be economic or political reasons for keeping it, but in the long term—if people don't become attached to it—it might not survive.

Our study of the Apulian landscape was instructive and valuable, but the landscape patterns that endure in Bari have limited value in and of themselves to landscape architects elsewhere. A piazza is a very effective design element in Mediterranean climates but is much less effective in, say, the Arctic. And the landscape patterns of the Inuit of the Arctic likely have little relevance or applicability in Bari. However, the underlying physical principles can be applied everywhere. It is this notion of principles based on theory that is the second main way to approach the design of climatic-ally appropriate places.

When Diane studied the heat flow in the piazza, she was considering the *energy budget* of the space. This same type of analysis can be done on any landscape or any object in a landscape, and it is what I used earlier to describe the flows of energy to and from a person. It turns out that it isn't the *patterns* in the landscape that can be transferred elsewhere; it is the *process* of modifying microclimate that is universally applicable.

This is contrary to the concept of style in architectural or landscape architectural design. When art deco was the prevailing style of architec-ture, the look influenced the design of buildings around the world. While driving around New Zealand a few years ago, I wandered into the city of Napier-Hastings. A whole commercial section was designed in art deco style. They had apparently had an earthquake that destroyed a large por-tion of the city, and architects had a heyday rebuilding it. The art deco style was not regionally specific, nor did it have any particular function in terms of microclimate modification, so it could be transferred virtually anywhere.

In contrast, microclimatic design has a function that depends on the prevailing climate. For example, the breezy, light, and airy style of build-ings and outdoor spaces that might create wonderful microclimates in southern California have no place in northern Canada. The spaces, indoors and out, would be uninhabitable.

Microclimate is *the* most important consideration in designing and building outdoor spaces, yet it is also *the* most difficult and challenging area to understand and apply. If we had decades to spare, we could just sit back and let vernacular patterns emerge. In some areas of the world, where the ancient patterns have not been destroyed, we can study and learn from them. But, in reality, landscape architects need to know at least a little about the climates of small spaces so that their designs can create positive, thermally comfortable places. Microclimate is the most important consid-eration in designing outdoor spaces because it affects virtually everything else. You think that visual aesthetics is more important? Even the most beautiful space in the world would have few people admiring and enjoying it if the microclimate were brutally hot or freezing cold. Maybe the ecological function of a landscape is more important? Every plant and animal in the landscape will survive only if it is in an appropriate microclimate. Energy conservation? Water management? Economics? Microclimate. Microclimate. Microclimate.

I know of a fellow who built a new home in the foothills of the Rocky Mountains in western Canada. He loved the view to the west so much that even his outdoor hot tub was located so he could gaze at the snow-capped mountains while soaking his weary bones. He stayed in the house for one year after building it, then sold it. He said that he decided to move on the day that the whitecaps in his hot tub broke over his head. The constant west wind was so much at odds with his whole house that it was essentially an unlivable environment. Fortunately for him, few people make their house-buying decisions based on microclimate. This property has had a steady stream of owners, every one of whom loves the view to the mountains, and especially loves the hot tub set in such a way that they can gaze at the snow-capped mountains while soaking their weary bones.

I once advised a farmer not to build his new home to the east of his hog barn. I told him that the winds would be predominantly from the westerly direction and that he would be bathed in a stream of invisible yet pungent smells most of the time. He reckoned that it would be too expensive to build it where I suggested because he would have to extend his road. He was back a year later looking for advice. What could he do to stop the smell that permeated his house? Unfortunately, all I could tell him was that the house shouldn't have been built downwind of the hog barn.

One year I skipped the Canadian winter to live in Adelaide, Australia. While Canada was experiencing a very cold, very snowy season, we were living through a record-breaking heat wave in Adelaide. For more than a fortnight, as they reported it in Australia, the maximum air temperature every day was above 35°C (95°F), and many of those days it hovered near 40°C (104°F). Despite these very high air temperatures, the air humidity was very low, so sitting in the shade could actually be quite pleasant. But step into the sun and you were risking permanent damage to your body!

Figure 1.4 These people really wanted to see and hear Germaine Greer talk in Adelaide, Australia. The air temperature hovered near 40°C (104°F), and there wasn't a cloud in sight. The solar radiation was so intense that these people opted to be farther away but comfortably in the shade of the palms.

The intensity of the radiation was so high that it almost took your breath away. It was during one of these extra-hot days that Germaine Greer, a well-known Australian author, gave a public outdoor reading. An extra-large open-walled tent was erected that provided her and a sizable audience with shade, but those who came a bit late were left out. Despite the fact that people really wanted to hear her speak, and they really wanted to be close enough to see her, even more important to the audience was to find some shade. The meager shade from some palms became an oasis (see figure 1.4).

While I was in Australia, I noticed that Waverley Park Stadium, a very large sports facility in Melbourne, was being torn down. I asked some of the locals about it, and they said that it was because of its terrible microclimate! Well, they didn't actually say *microclimate*, but that's what they meant. They said that it had the nickname "Arctic Park" because even if the weather was favorable elsewhere, it was terrible in and around Waverley Park. The players and fans alike often had to endure wet, windy, cold conditions during games. The locals told me that nobody was very sad to see it go.

I've seen many houses and apartments in Tucson, Arizona, with west-facing windows that have been covered in aluminum foil to keep out the hot afternoon sun. I've seen beautiful overhead trellises built on the north sides of buildings where they never see the sun and are never used. I've seen rows of tall evergreen trees on the south side of buildings that effectively block the low winter sun, ensuring that the house and yard will be dark and cold all winter but allowing the high summer sun to bake the house and yard. I've seen evergreen windbreaks where someone had removed the lower branches, thereby not only allowing cold winter winds to blow underneath but in fact forcing the wind to speed up as it squeezes through the opening. None of these things was done on purpose, and all could have been easily avoided through a basic understanding of microclimatic design principles.

So why do so many people choose to ignore microclimate? Why do we end up with so many uncomfortable, unenduring landscapes? I suggest two main reasons: first, there is little public demand for microclimatic design because people in general don't know what's possible, and second, it's hard for designers to consider microclimate because of the need to understand the underlying science.

Does any of this explain why we boys were so comfortable when squatting on the south side of the house but so cold everywhere else in the yard?

It was simply that we were sitting in an area that was shielded from the wind and in the full sun. This meant that our convective heat loss was small despite the air temperature being quite a bit lower than our skin temperature, and we were absorbing large amounts of solar radiation. Out in the wind, our convective cooling was extremely high because not only was the wind moving quite fast but we were often running *into* the wind, which made the relative wind speed even higher. We were maximizing the number of cold air molecules that could come in contact with our bodies (particularly our fingers, ears, and lips, all of which had no external insulating layer). Within a short time, we couldn't supply enough energy to those exposed appendages, and they were starting to get very cold.

I hope you will find the anecdotes and historical tidbits in this book useful in bringing microclimate to life for you—to allow you to see this important yet invisible component of the landscape. There is nothing to memorize and no difficult formulas to try to master—just a series of stories about many different aspects of microclimate and some principles and concepts for considering microclimate in design.

In the end, I hope that you will develop a deep understanding of the landscape-microclimate system and will understand clearly how to design successful, thermally comfortable outdoor places for people.

2

VERNACULAR

Think for a minute about what it would be like to live before the discovery of fossil fuels. It would be a lot more challenging than just giving up some modern conveniences. It would probably be a lot like camping year-round—except that you would have to cook everything over a wood fire. And you couldn't load up your car and drive home if it started to rain or when winter rolled around. But this is essentially the way people lived until the past few generations. They had to find a good way to fit in with their climatic environment or they simply didn't survive.

Humans are remarkably resourceful, though, and our ancestors were able to develop ways to survive quite nicely in every environment on earth. Want to live in the desert, the tundra, or the jungle? No problem. People found ways to work within the limits and constraints of their environments. If it was really hot for part of the year, they didn't have the option to install central air. Instead, they figured out ways to stay cool by creating thermally comfortable microclimates. However, after the discovery of fossil fuels, the need to fit a building into the local climatic environment became less important. Buildings could be constructed with a central heating and air-conditioning system that allowed the interior to be climate controlled and thus thermally comfortable at all times. As a result, many of the traditional ways of staying comfortable have been lost or forgotten.

But a lot can be learned by looking at the way people used to live in different climatic regions. And there are many traditional patterns on the land that we can analyze, many of which still exist in various forms. In many ways, the landscape is like a *palimpsest*—an ancient parchment that was written on, then erased and written on again. Grocery lists got erased, while important or valuable information survived. In the landscape, if someone tried a technique for making their home environment more comfortable or their fields more productive and it failed, it would have been erased. Landscapes that are microclimatically appropriate tend to survive and offer much that can be learned. In this chapter, we'll browse a few examples of patterns on the landscape that have persisted, and we'll try to elucidate some of the reasons they succeeded.

The first desert traveler who spent a night in a south-facing cave probably found it to be a good place. Based on the number of surviving examples, it apparently became accepted practice for people living in the Sonora Desert in North America to live in caves (see figure 2.1).

Winters in the caves would have been toasty warm with solar radiation streaming in from the low-in-the-sky sun, while summers would have been pleasantly cool with solar radiation from the high-in-the-sky sun blocked by the overhanging rock. The cool winter winds were blocked by the sides of the cave. The thick rock walls buffered the cold in the winter and the heat in the summer.

People no longer live in these places, but they have inspired many design instructors to use principles based on these early residences in their lectures. They tell their students that buildings should have most of their windows on the south side and that each window should have a long overhang above it. This allows the sun to enter and warm the interior during the winter, and the overhang keeps the solar radiation out in the hot summer. Few windows should be on the east, north, and west walls, and all walls should be well insulated. The design of houses can vary greatly as long as these basic principles are followed. For example, the Arthur Brown house in Tucson, Arizona, has almost all the windows on the south face,

Figure 2.1 This ancient cave dwelling in Arizona is on the south-facing slope of a cliff. People found it to be a very livable environment in the midst of a hot desert climate.

and there is a movable structure that can be rolled around to strategically shade areas in the house and yard (see figure 2.2). During cool winter days, the sun streams in through the south-facing windows, bathing the interior of the house. On hot summer days, the sun is kept out of the house by the overhang and the movable shading devices, leaving the house shady and cool. Similarly, the living space just outside the sliding glass doors on the south side of the house is a very pleasant place to be almost any day of the year.

The people living on the North American plains when European settlers arrived had finely tuned their living environments to fit into the harsh continental climate. In the area currently known as Saskatchewan,

Figure 2.2 This modern-style house in Tucson, Arizona, is very climatically appropriate with a long overhang and floor-to-ceiling windows on the south side. This photograph was taken on a cool day in January, and you can see that the solar radiation is streaming into the house. The north side of the house has only very small windows.

the people of the plains lived in portable homes called tipis. These structures were made of animal skins laid over a framework of stout poles to form a conelike shape. There was an entry flap that would open on one side, and an opening at the top to allow smoke to exit. During the winter, both the opening at the top and the entry flap would be oriented away from the wind, and the entry flap would be tightly closed except to allow entry and exit. As the wind passed over the top of the tipi, it drew smoke from the top opening but didn't flow in. During summer, the opening was oriented toward the wind but the flap was oriented away from the wind and was often left at least partly open. This combination allowed wind to enter the opening at the top, flow down through the tipi, and exit through the lower flap, cooling and ventilating the tipi.

During the summer, tipis were located on tops of hills to capture the most wind possible. As wind moves up and over a hill, it is forced to compress slightly as the ground rises, and the speed of the wind increases. The windiest spot in the landscape is often at the crest of a hill, and this is where the tipis were often located. Not only did this provide increased ventilation and cooling, but it also helped to ward off the scourge of the prairies—mosquitoes! These stinging insects cannot maneuver well in wind, so they hide in the grass until the wind abates. A fairly constant wind ensures a reasonably mosquito-free time.

If you have an opportunity to wander through the hills of southwestern Saskatchewan on lands that have not been turned into cropland, you will almost certainly come upon tipi rings on the tops of the hills. The edges of tipis were held down with rocks, and when the tipi was moved the rocks remained in a circle. Standing among these tipi rings, you come to realize some of the other advantages of living on the crests of hills—such as the spectacular views and the ability to receive ample advance warning in the case of an enemy attack.

Smack dab in the middle of the remarkably flat glacial lake bed that provides Saskatchewan with its reputation as a flat province is the First Nations University. Housed in a building designed by Douglas Cardinal, it sports many indigenous characteristics. One very clever and effective design feature is the way overhangs were provided over south-facing windows. Cardinal used the floor above (see figure 2.3)!

There are many other areas in the world where people are still living with ancient patterns that can be analyzed. The traces are particularly strong in Japan, a land where traditions are celebrated and ancient patterns persist through cultural and social celebrations.

Japan has a long history of caring about design. Flower arranging, for example, is a high art form that follows a set of unbreakable and incomprehensible (to me) rules. The art form is called *ikebana* and has its roots in the sixth century (!). One ikebana school can trace its recorded history

Figure 2.3 The First Nations University building in Regina has its floors offset so that the south-facing windows are shaded in summer and allow solar radiation to penetrate the building in winter.

back to 1462. In Japan, design is not a trend; it is an institution. And it goes beyond flowers—virtually every part of Japanese life is carefully and thoroughly designed. Visiting the famous gardens of Kyoto is an interesting experience for foreigners. Actually just visiting Japan in general is mind-bending.

Before my first visit to Japan, I dutifully learned a few words and phrases in Japanese so I would be able to converse with the locals. All through the long flight over the north of Canada and down the Kamchatka Peninsula, I practiced my *konichiwa* and *sayonara* and thought I was really doing something when I could say without stumbling *domo arigato gozai-masu.* I expected to be saying that a lot since it means "thank you very much." However, it wasn't until too late that I realized that I should also have learned to say *yukkuri hanashite kudasai*, which means "please speak slowly."

Fortunately for me, quite a few Japanese people, especially in Tokyo, know how to speak a little English and are anxious to do two things: help tourists and practice their English. Stand on a street corner with a map in your hand looking helpless and within seconds someone will come up and offer to help.

This helped me on numerous occasions and allowed me to meet a lot of Japanese. Through these broken English conversations, I learned much about the people and the culture. People stopped me on the street to point out a flower that had just bloomed. Or to make sure that I took the time to listen to a bird singing in a tree. They seemed so aware of the beauty in the environment—even everyday environments.

Through research projects over the years, I have managed to see much of rural Japan. By visiting ancient villages and farms. I've been able to observe the traditional patterns on the land—the palimpsest of the Japanese landscape.

One project was a book that I coedited with some Japanese colleagues on the traditional rural landscape of Japan known as the *satoyama*. The book focused primarily on the agricultural and land use patterns and how they have changed over time, but the patterns are also instructive in terms of microclimatic design. They illustrate the powerful role of the micro-climatologic concept of *orientation*.

Satoyama landscapes throughout Japan have a clearly identifiable pattern. The ideal satoyama has forested hills or mountains on the north, with the settlement on the south-facing lower slopes. To the south of the settlement is the area reserved for dry field crops, and to the south of this are the paddy fields. Oak trees on the hills are regularly harvested about every ten years through coppicing. The stumps sprout at the base and grow stout stalks that are ready to be cut again in another ten years. The houses to the south of the hills have good access to solar radiation in the cool winter months, when the sun is low in the sky. The satoyama landscape provides a system by which people can live sustainably on and use the land over a very long period of time. Everything in their lives is adapted to the micro-climate—especially the homes.

Traditional houses in Japan respond well to microclimate through their orientation and design. More than seven hundred years ago, the *Tsurezure-gusa* (roughly translated as *Essays in Idleness*) provided advice on house design that is still being followed today. The *Tsurezuregusa* suggested that homes in Japan should be designed to deal primarily with the hot, humid summers and that designers shouldn't worry too much about designing for wintertime. Winters will take care of themselves. Houses are traditionally heavy, timber-framed buildings with walls that can be slid open or closed. In the hot summer, the houses are opened to allow air movement, while in winter they are closed to keep out the cold. Oversized roofs keep out both the rain and the sun during the summer but allow solar radiation to stream into the interior during the cool winters.

When I travel in rural Japan, I like to stay in small local inns known as *ryokans* (the *r* is almost silent, so it is pronounced like *yo-con*, with no emphasis on either syllable). There are some wonderful but bewildering ceremonies that must be followed when checking in to a ryokan. The signing of the register is a fairly long and formal event that involves drinking several cups of green tea while sitting on the floor around a low table. On one of my stays, it was winter and the house had been designed, as the *Tsurezuregusa* suggested, for summer time. Many of the walls were made of rice paper, and the interior of the house was quite cool, almost cold. We crossed our legs and put our knees under the table, and I noticed that everyone was pulling the edge of the table covering to their waists so I followed suit. At this point, I became aware of a small heater under the table. The heat was kept under the table by the heavy cloth, so only a small amount of energy was needed to warm this small space. Once my legs were in that space, I was toasty warm from my waist down. The hot tea heated my core, and I have to say that I was remarkably comfortable despite the cool interior of the room. In addition, the sun was shining into the space, brightening it up and warming surfaces through absorption of solar radiation. Rather than heating the whole space, the strategic heating of only the people was very energy efficient and very comfortable.

When I spent a term as visiting professor at the University of Tokyo, I joined a group of graduate students on a field study of the gardens of Kyoto. Of course, the garden at the top of our list was Ryo-an-ji (again the r is almost silent, so it sounds more like *yo-on-jee*, with no emphasis on any of the syllables). Volumes have been written about the garden's subtle beauty and its ability to inspire people to meditate and become at peace with themselves.

The garden at Ryo-an-ji Temple in Kyoto is ancient by anyone's standard. There has apparently been a temple on the site since about 983, and the last redesign of the garden took place in about 1488. Nothing much has changed since then—except that now it has become a superstar and everyone wants to see it.

Every day, people from throughout Japan and around the world flock to Ryo-an-ji, pay the five-dollar admission fee, and then sit and gaze out over a ten-by-thirty-meter white gravel pad that has some bigger rocks jutting through.

My first impression was of a very simple, very elegant garden (see figure 2.4). I was immediately struck by the feel of the place. People were sitting along the edge serenely gazing at carefully raked gravel and islands of rocks. The primary function of the garden and the adjacent building was originally to provide a place for monks to reproduce manuscripts. They would sit for long hours, cross-legged on a tatami mat, and copy documents by hand. They had to do this year-round, so they required a place that had sufficient light, was thermally comfortable, and had a contemplative environment.

The buildings were oriented to the south to allow sunlight to enter the room during cool winter days. As in many Japanese structures, the walls were movable, and the south wall of the building could be opened completely to allow total access to the garden. The garden to the south of the

Figure 2.4　The temple garden of Ryo-an-ji Temple in Kyoto, Japan. The dry landscape garden is one of the most famous gardens in the world.

building was covered with white gravel that would allow solar radiation to be reflected into the room. The sunlight was important both to warm the monks and to provide light so they could see what they were writing. The white gravel was susceptible to growing moss and becoming covered with leaves or other debris, all of which would reduce the amount of reflected light, so the monks would regularly rake the gravel to ensure that the surface was as clean and light colored as possible (see figure 2.5). This raking became an art form in itself, as the rakers began to create patterns in the gravel. These patterns change with each raker, as well as with the mood of the raker.

Trees were kept out of the garden to keep from blocking the important sunlight or dropping leaves on the gravel. A wall delimited the garden,

Figure 2.5   The light-colored gravel in dry landscape gardens is raked into patterns.

partly because of the space restrictions but also to reduce the winds in the winter. The more calm the air during the cool periods, the more comfortable for people living and working there. The wall also played an important role during summer. Cool air could "pool" in the garden and would not flow out. Also, for summertime conditions, a large overhanging roof was built over the platform on the south side in front of the writing room. The high sun angle during summer meant that the whole writing space was shaded. The white gravel reflected much of the solar radiation reaching the garden, so the input of solar radiation was greatly reduced and the garden was kept cooler. A person standing in the garden would receive a very high radiation load on a sunny summer day, but the only people allowed into the garden are the monks who rake and maintain it, and they complete their work in the early morning before the heat of the day.

Once the basic layout of the garden was determined based on function and microclimate, a framework was established within which individual monks or orders of monks could apply their creativity. They had many hours to contemplate the space and decide where to locate rocks, how to rake the gravel, and so on. The microclimate determined the framework within which is now one of the most wonderful places in the world.

After participating in an academic conference in Lima one January (deep cold winter in Ontario, midsummer in Peru), I traveled from Lima to the city of Cusco, high in the Andes mountains. The elevation of this ancient Incan community is so high that many people get altitude sickness when they arrive. It can take the body a few days to acclimatize to the lower levels of oxygen in the air, a process aided by drinking the completely legal and therapeutic coca leaf tea. After the requisite days of rest, I took the train to Machu Picchu, the ancient and mysterious ruins high in the Andes.

The train left the station very early in the morning while it was still dark. As our train pulled out of Cusco, it traveled for about five minutes, then stopped and returned to the station. Once back at the station, we stopped and headed off again in the same direction as we had the first time, only to stop again five minutes later and return to the station once more. It turns out that Cusco is surrounded by mountains with slopes that are too steep for trains to go straight up. So the train has to leave the city by zigzagging back and forth, each time on a different track, gradually gaining elevation, until finally it can leave the basin.

After a surprisingly long train ride, we disembarked in a small village and made our way to a waiting bus. The bus then crawled up the side of the mountain, switchback after switchback, each one offering a more magnificent view and more than a few sweaty palms. Finally, after a seemingly precarious ride, we arrived at the parking area. From there we hiked up some very steep paths until finally we emerged into the open and could see Machu Picchu at our feet. The view was magnificent. Even if there were no ruins there, it would be worth seeing the precipitous drops and tree-covered slopes (see figure 2.6).

Figure 2.6 It's a long and difficult trek to Machu Picchu, but it's definitely worth the effort.

Machu Picchu is located near the equator, so you would expect it to be very hot, but because of the high elevation the air temperature does not get very high. Despite the fact that the air temperature hovered around 15°C (59°F) that day, however, people were not wearing jackets or sweaters. There was a large input of solar radiation, and after hiking around the ruins for a short while people began to seek out cooler places. At one point, after I had climbed high above the ruins, I looked down to see that almost everyone was in the shade of a single tree (see figure 2.7).

Despite being in one of the most magnificent and interesting land-scapes on earth, and despite having made an arduous trip that would likely be once in a lifetime, people quit exploring the ruins and gravitated to the one spot on the site where the solar radiation load was reduced to a

Figure 2.7 Visitors to the ancient city of Machu Picchu take a break. The air temperature was low, but almost everyone was looking for a spot in the shade.

thermally comfortable level: under the tree. To me, this served as a powerful indication of the value of microclimate.

One of my graduate students, Nimmi, spent some time in India collecting data for her thesis. Not having been to India myself, I was very interested to hear what she had found out about how the locals deal with the intense heat in the middle of the dry season. One of the most poignant stories she told me was about people going to outdoor prayers in the heat of the day. Some days the temperature can reach 50°C (122°F) with full sun and no wind—a recipe for hyperthermia! Nimmi described the apparatus that had been set up to protect the worshippers. The first element was a series of bolts of thin white cloth hung horizontally overhead. This intercepted and reflected away much of the solar radiation before it reached the people. The second element was a series of overhead pipes with small nozzles on them that sprayed a very fine mist of water. Before the water reached the people, or perhaps just as it reached their skin, it evaporated. Water requires quite a large amount of energy to change states from liquid to gaseous form, and in this case it would take that energy either from the air or from the skin of the people. In either case, it provided a cooler environment. The air was being cooled, and the skin surfaces of the people were being cooled. The very dry air in India during the dry season allows for tremendous amounts of evaporative cooling to take place.

There has been much inadvertent modification of microclimates in history as well. Some of these changes might have contributed to the demise of some civilizations, and some of them we are only now attempting to address. A couple of big issues that remain to be resolved are *urban heat islands* and *air pollution*.

Cities tend to replace vegetated landscapes with concrete and asphalt—soft, moist, and green becomes hard, dry, and gray. The result is an urban core that is hotter and drier than the surrounding countryside and that has become known as an urban heat island. Some cities have very little urban vegetation (see figure 2.8) and can create situations where the air temperature in the core of the city is several degrees warmer than outside the city. This effect is most prevalent on clear evenings when natural areas have an opportunity to cool down but urban areas do not.

Another urban scourge is air pollution. Exhaust from vehicles, furnaces, power-generating plants, and manufacturing all contribute by spewing particles and gases, such as sulphur oxide, nitrogen oxide, and carbon monoxide, into the air. This causes problems ranging from damaged structures to health issues in the population. These problems are often experienced not in the area where the pollutants are generated but some distance downwind. Smog is often worse downwind from a city than it is in the city

Figure 2.8 Lima, Peru, is a vast, sprawling city with almost no green spaces. The predominance of hard surfaces creates an urban climate that is warmer and drier than surrounding countryside. A similar situation occurs in large cities around the world.

itself. It's a bit like living downstream from someone who insists on running their sewer into the waterway. They have little incentive to change since there is little personal consequence.

In one situation in Canada, air pollution from the nickel refinery in Sudbury was killing the local vegetation. The landscape was so devoid of life that NASA trained their astronauts there for going to the moon. The situation was resolved by building a much taller stack for the emissions, and the local environment around Sudbury has rebounded spectacularly. But all they really did was move the problem farther afield so that it no longer was Sudbury's problem. Now the emissions are being scattered downwind of the city and dispersed over a larger area.

Whether a landscape or a building modifies the microclimate in a positive or negative manner, there is much that it can teach us. Human creativity and ingenuity are boundless, and our ancestors were faced with living in some very challenging climatic conditions. Their creative solutions are slowly but surely disappearing and should be documented and studied before they go. There is probably an example near you that could be studied. Is there a very old house that was built before central heating and air-conditioning became popular? Maybe it has been built in a manner that minimizes the energy use. Maybe there is a shelterbelt of trees that protects it from the prevailing cold winds during winter. Maybe there is some enigmatic element in the house, like a hollow wall, or a stack with a scoop that you could investigate and figure out its purpose. Or maybe there is an abandoned apple orchard near your home. Maybe the location relative to the topography is interesting. What direction is the slope facing? Are there some trees still alive while others have died? Are there different varieties of apples in different parts of the orchard? These might be clues as to the microclimatic conditions. There are examples all around us, and all we need to do is to look for them.

3

COMPONENTS

A few years ago, I provided some professional advice on a hospital that was being planned in a snowy climate. The footprint of the hospital had been tentatively laid out, and I estimated the likely amount and location of snow deposition during a typical snowstorm. The location that would likely have the highest deposition of snow was right at the ambulance and emergency room entrance to the hospital. If the hospital had been built as planned, this would have created an ongoing maintenance problem for the life of the hospital—and could potentially have put people's lives at risk. It's a simple but poignant example of why microclimate should be considered early in the design process—before major decisions about location and orientation are made. In this chapter, we are going to learn about each of the components of the energy budget and consider ways that each can be understood and modified by the landscape.

There is a game that we sometimes play at faculty retreats to get things rolling. Each person in turn tells two true things about themselves and one lie. Everyone else has to guess which statement is the lie. It has led to some interesting insights about our colleagues and their lives before academia!

Let's play the same game now using statements about microclimate. Before we do this, though, let's broaden our understanding of microclimate to include not only flows of energy but also atmospheric characteristics, such as the composition of the air and the movement of sound through the air.

43

Here are three statements, two of which are true and one of which is a lie. Can you spot the lie? 1. Trees cause air pollution. 2. Ozone damages plants. 3. Trees reduce noise. There might seem to be at least two lies in the group. Trees are well known for removing pollution from the air, right? How could they cause it? And we hear about the ozone layer all the time and how important it is to preserve it—but it's high up in the atmosphere. How could it damage plants? The only one you might be sure of is that vegetation reduces noise in the landscape because we see it used that way all the time.

Well, just like at our faculty meetings, the things that seem to be obviously true are actually lies, and sometimes the obvious lies turn out to be true. Consider the statement about trees causing air pollution. You were right in thinking that in some cases trees can remove small amounts of pollution from the air, but in many cases trees actually contribute to air pollution in urban environments. When trees open the stomata on their leaves to take in oxygen, they give off, among other things, hydrocarbons. On warm sunny days, these emissions combine with nitrogen oxide from the exhaust of automobiles to create pollution. Certain trees, such as poplars and willows, are particularly big offenders, while other trees, such as oaks and maples, are less problematic. But the fact can't be avoided: trees cause air pollution! So when landscape architects are considering which species of trees to plant in urban areas, they need to take into account the effect the trees will have on the composition of the air.

What about the second statement, the one about ozone? Well, ozone in the upper atmosphere intercepts a wavelength of solar radiation that is dangerous to life on earth. The depletion of this ozone is causing serious problems on earth in several ways, not the least of which is that it is making it dangerous for people to be outdoors on sunny days. However, ozone also occurs at the surface of the earth as an air pollutant—and is therefore a component of the microclimate. When plants open the stomata on their leaves to take a breath, ozone enters the plant and can cause serious damage. Some plants are more susceptible than others, with some grain crops suffering serious damage. So, when landscape architects are working in areas known to have ground-level ozone problems, they have to be selective in the plants that they use, choosing those that are not susceptible to ozone damage.

For those of you keeping track, this means that the first two statements are true, so the third one must be a lie. Trees are often planted alongside sources of noise pollution, but in fact they have very little effect. Even fairly dense plantings have only a minimal effect. And, a very weird situation occurs in the atmosphere that can completely remove even the smallest benefit of vegetation. Consider people living near a busy highway. Arguably the majority of those people would want the noise of the highway to be decreased in the evenings and at night when they are at home, and they might not care too much about how much noise there is during the day when they are away from home at work or school. On clear evenings, when you might want to sit out in your backyard and listen to the crickets chirp, something called an *inversion* can occur in the atmosphere. Normally, the air temperature decreases with height above the surface, but on clear nights the surface can cool down rapidly and will cool the air next to it as well. This can create a situation where the air temperature increases with height for a while and then falls off normally above that point. The point in the atmosphere where the temperature stops rising and starts to fall off will reflect noise and cause it to be diverted back down toward the surface. This basically allows the noise to skip over any barrier of vegetation, as if it weren't there. So, in this case, the vegetation provides no barrier at all to the noise of the highway. The bottom line is that when considering the noise-distribution aspect of the microclimate in areas near highways, landscape architects cannot count on vegetation to provide much of a sound buffer.

There are many more counterintuitive situations related to microclimate. Using intuition alone, it would seem reasonable to plant trees in urban areas to absorb pollution; in order to have a fairly immediate effect, you might put in fast-growing trees such as poplar or willow—and you would, in fact, cause an increase in pollution levels. Landscape architects can't afford to be amateur microclimatologists, trusting their intuition in matters of microclimate—they will be wrong much of the time. And it isn't just a benign effect. They can actually make the situation worse—much worse. Unfortunately, much of what happens in the physics of the atmosphere and the way that it interacts with the landscape is not what you might expect. I can tell you about some of the situations, but I think it is much more effective if you understand the basic mechanisms by which microclimates work. That way your intuition will be well informed. I suggest that we start with the big picture.

BIG PICTURE

The sun provides virtually all the energy that fuels the atmosphere. However, radiation from the sun passes through a clear sky almost as if it weren't there. Only a very small portion of the radiation is absorbed or reflected by the air before it reaches the ground, and most of the absorbed radiation would be dangerous to humans if it were allowed through (like that absorbed by the ozone layer). Clouds in the sky will intercept and reflect a lot of solar radiation, but the key point here is that the sun does not heat the atmosphere directly. Instead, solar radiation falls on the earth, where some is absorbed by the molecules that make up the landscape. Darker-colored surfaces will absorb more solar radiation than lighter-colored surfaces, which is the main reason that asphalt gets so much hotter on a sunny day than concrete does. Molecules that absorb solar radiation get excited by the input of energy, and their temperature rises. Air molecules are in constant contact with the earth, and some of this energy is transferred to them, making them warmer as well. An individual air molecule at the surface of the earth can move only about one millionth of a centimeter before it collides with another air molecule.[1]

Needless to say, there are a lot of collisions, and there is a lot of energy being transferred. Air molecules that are warmed through contact with the earth become lighter and rise up through the cooler and heavier air molecules around them. As each warmed particle rises, a cooler particle falls into its place and also gets warmed by the earth, becomes lighter, and rises as well. As molecules move up through a dry atmosphere, they cool at a pretty consistent rate of about 1°C for every one hundred meters of vertical distance (about 0.5°F for every one hundred feet); if the air is moist, the rate is about 0.6°C for every one hundred meters (about 0.3°F for every one hundred feet).

This is an important relationship for landscape architects to keep in mind for several reasons. For example, when a design project is undertaken, one valuable piece of background information is the typical air temperature at different times of day and in different seasons. If the data that you acquire is from a weather station that is at a different elevation than your study site, it needs to be adjusted—sometimes quite a lot. For example, the weather station at Cranbrook, British Columbia, is at the airport, whose elevation is 930 meters (3,050 feet), but my summer home in Kimberley, British Columbia, which is less than twenty kilometers (about 12 miles) away, is at an elevation of 1,300 meters (4,270 feet), a difference of 370 meters (1,220 feet). When the air temperature at the weather station is 20°C (68°F), the air temperature at my place would be nearer to 16.3°C (61.3°F)—quite a difference!

In another example, I was involved in the microclimatic design of the rooftop of a tall building in Manhattan (more on that later). The rooftop is about 280 meters (750 feet) above the ground, so climate data from the Central Park weather station had to be adjusted lower by more than 2°C (3.6°F).

Tucked away in the southwest corner of Saskatchewan is an upland area known as the Cypress Hills.[2] Driving from the prairie town of Maple Creek to the hills less than twenty-five kilometers (fifteen miles) away, the elevation rises more than six hundred meters (about two thousand feet). And, indeed, the air temperature drops by about 6°C (about 10°F) during the climb. A hot summer day on the prairies becomes a cool springlike day at Cypress.

Another terrific road to drive and experience the relationship between elevation and air temperature is in Tucson, Arizona. One hot spring day when the air temperature in Tucson was about 30°C (86°F), we drove up Mount Lemmon, a rise of about 2,000 meters (6,500 feet), which can be done in about an hour. As you drive, you pass through different climate zones as the air temperature drops. When we reached the top, it was about 10°C (50°F), and there was still snow lying in patches on the shady north sides of hills.

AIR TEMPERATURE

Every year I give many talks about microclimate and how it can be modified through design. I often talk about some of the oddities and counterintuitive aspects of microclimate, and I find that people are generally pretty interested and accepting of my information. However, there is one thing in particular that I tell my audiences that many people find hard to believe. Despite the fact that I provide scientific evidence, most of the comments and questions after my talks focus on the apparently unbelievable information that I am going to share with you now. Here it is. *If you move expeditiously through a landscape carrying a thermometer at about chest height, the air temperature readings will be almost identical wherever you go.*

At first this might seem obvious, but then you might think about a hot day when you walked from the full sun into the shade and found that it was much cooler. If I were in the audience, I might think of a parking lot on a hot sunny day. All of the parking spots in the shade would be full, so I would have to park in the full sun. I would step out of my car, and it would be hot, very hot. I would walk past the cars parked in the shade, and it would be so much cooler. Surely the air temperature is a lot higher in the sun than in the shade.

Well, there is no question that a person would *feel* hotter in the sunny part of the parking lot than in the shade. However, what you feel in terms of your thermal comfort is not dependent on the air temperature alone. Other things are also affecting what you sense, and often these other factors have a much more powerful influence on your comfort than does the air temperature.

Air temperature is one of only a small number of things that need to be measured in order to describe a microclimate, and you hear about them all every day. Weather forecasters will report on the air temperature, relative humidity, wind, sun and cloud coverage, and precipitation. These are all very familiar concepts, but they are far from easy things to measure. For example, measuring the temperature of the air is a very tricky business.

When Daniel Fahrenheit started making thermometers in the early 1700s, there was no standard size for a degree and there was no general agreement on where the scale on the instrument should stop and start. He put his early thermometers into the mouths of healthy men and labeled that point as 22.5°F. He then put the thermometers into ice water and labeled that value as 7.5°F. He apparently saw the difficulty in using a scale such as this, so he multiplied all the values by four, which yielded a temperature of 90°F for the core temperature of people, and 30°F as the temperature at which water freezes. He then reasoned that it would be more convenient to have 64 degrees between body temperature and ice water rather than 60°, as 64 is divisible by 2 without leading to fractions. So he set the temperature at which water freezes to the now familiar 32°F, and the temperature of human cores to 96°F. After his death, it became normal to calibrate thermometers using the boiling point of water (which was 212°F on his scale) and the freezing point of water. These were more stable values than the core temperature of people, which can vary somewhat from person to person.

Not long after this, Anders Celsius came up with a much more rational and easy-to-understand scale where water freezes at 0°C and boils at 100°C. Old habits die hard, though, and some parts of the world, including the United States, still use the awkward Fahrenheit scale. Thermometers now come in many types and sizes and give quick and easy readings. However, the challenging part is to tell what it is they are really measuring.

Let's start by considering how a simple mercury-in-glass thermometer works. Mercury changes volume with temperature, expanding as it warms and contracting as it cools, but it remains liquid even in the coldest weather.[3] This makes it an ideal material for use in thermometers. When the mercury in the reservoir at the bottom of the thermometer gets warmer, it expands and forces some mercury to move up the tiny tube running up the middle. We can see the height of the mercury in the thermometer and read the number on the scale. Mercury expands and contracts with temperature at a very well-known, consistent rate. However, it is difficult to get exactly the same amount of mercury into every thermometer. It is also difficult to make every glass thermometer exactly the same size, with the same size reservoir and with the same size tube in the middle of the glass. So if we were to line up a dozen thermometers and put them into the same environment, we might get a dozen slightly different readings. If we used good-quality instruments, the readings would be pretty close but they likely wouldn't be identical. So this is problem number one. How do we get all thermometers to read the same value?

Well, if you live in Canada, you could take the instrument to Ottawa and compare it with the national standard, which in turn has been compared with the international standard. I bought a new thermometer a few years ago and sent it to Ottawa for calibration. They put my thermometer and the national standard thermometer into a range of predefined environments and compared the readings. It turned out that my thermometer reads a little high—that is, when my thermometer says 19.8°C (67.64°F), the true temperature is 19.7°C (67.46°F). So every time I take measurements with that thermometer, I have to subtract a tenth of a degree (0.18°F) to get the real temperature.

Once you have a thermometer that you can count on to give accurate and precise values, you can think about using it to measure the air temperature. If you just held it in your hand and walked out into the landscape, you would get a reading. This reading, however, would not actually represent the temperature of the air but would instead be the result of a combination of many different factors. Heat from your hand would be transferred to the mercury, causing it to expand. Radiation from the sun and the surrounding environment would be absorbed by the mercury, also causing it to expand. Wind might cool the thermometer through convection, causing the mercury to contract. Each of these would affect the volume of the mercury, and if you were to just read the level of mercury in the tube, you would be measuring not the temperature of the air but some combination of many factors. Yikes!

Think for a minute about the big thermometers that people often put in their yards—you know, the ones that have a deer jumping over a fence printed in the background. People often hang them in locations where the sun falls on them for at least part of the day, and they gleefully report things like "it was 35°C (95°F) in the sun today." The reading of a thermometer in the sun will undoubtedly be high, much higher than the weather forecast, but you can see now that the weather forecast was predicting air temperature, while the jumping-deer thermometer would be measuring some combination of air temperature plus solar radiation plus heat from the building plus who knows what else.

Lots of people, including some researchers, make this mistake, and unfortunately there is quite a bit of literature that uses erroneous air temperature measurements. Watch for it when you are reading books and journals. They will draw conclusions that would not be supported by correctly measured data. ,

So how could you possibly take a true measurement of the temperature of the air? Basically, what you have to do is to make sure that the thermometer is measuring only the temperature of the air and that there is no possibility that the instrument is being affected by any other sources of energy. You can do this by making sure that enough air is passing over the thermometer to allow the thermometer and the air to reach a thermal equilibrium. If the air is a bit warmer than the thermometer, then heat will be transferred from the air molecules to the thermometer. If the air is a bit cooler than the thermometer, then heat will be transferred from the thermometer to the air molecules. When no heat is passing either way, the resulting measurement of the thermometer will be a measure of the air temperature.

The air has to be moving quickly enough that it overwhelms the effects of things that would heat up the instrument, such as solar radiation. There are a variety of ways that this can be done, but in general the thermometer needs to be *shielded from the sun* and *well ventilated*. One early proponent of accurate air temperature measurement was Thomas Stevenson, father of the famous author Robert Louis Stevenson. He invented an instrument stand that is now known as the Stevenson Screen. It's a common sight at climate stations and airports—a white box with slatted sides set at about chest height. The white box reflects much of the solar radiation and keeps it from reaching the thermometer, while the slatted sides allow the wind to pass through. Over the years, we've found that this is a good solution but not perfect, as there can still be some radiation error.

A more effective way to measure the air temperature is to put a good-quality thermometer inside a tube that is covered with white paint or aluminum foil, which will reflect a large portion of the solar radiation that falls on it. Put a fan in the other end of the tube and turn it on so that it *pulls* air through the tube and past the thermometer. Using a system like this allows you to take measurements of air temperature that are accurate to about a tenth of a degree or less.

If you used a system like this, you would find that air temperatures throughout a landscape would be virtually identical at any one given point in time (see figure 3.1). Some researchers recently set up a carefully controlled experiment in a sunny parking lot on a hot day. They measured the air temperature over asphalt that was in full sun and over asphalt that was in the shade of a tree. This is certainly a situation where you would expect to see large differences in temperature because if you were to stand in those two places you would surely feel a big difference in your comfort level. When they measured the ground *surfaces*, they found that the asphalt in the sun was 20°C (36°F) hotter than that in the shade. However, when they took measurements of the air temperature at 1.5 meters *above the sur-*

Figure 3.1 If this person has a thermometer that records the true air temperature, then the reading he takes in the shade of the tree will be virtually identical to the reading in the full sun. The difference in his apparent thermal comfort level will be caused by other factors, including the amount of solar radiation falling on his body, and not by differences in air temperature.

face, the values in the two places were virtually identical. The air temperatures were within half a degree of each other, and even that difference might have been due to radiation error.

Now, I have to admit to you that I was pretty careful in wording my initial statement: *If you move expeditiously through a landscape carrying a thermometer at about chest height, the air temperature readings will be almost identical wherever you go.* The key words are 'expeditiously', 'landscape', and 'chest height'. Air temperature will change over time, over long distances, and with height. But if we hold those variables constant, then there are generally very small differences in air temperature.

There are a few times and places where the relationship is not completely true, and these situations can be used effectively in microclimate modification. They occur in situations where there is little or no mixing of the air—in areas or times where it is almost completely calm. For example, on clear nights, surfaces exposed to the open sky can cool down and the air

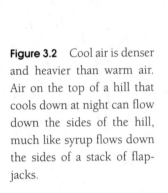

Figure 3.2 Cool air is denser and heavier than warm air. Air on the top of a hill that cools down at night can flow down the sides of the hill, much like syrup flows down the sides of a stack of flapjacks.

next to the surface will cool down as well. If this happens on a hilltop, the cooler air, which is heavier than the warmer air around it, will flow down the hillside just like maple syrup flows down the side of a stack of pancakes (see figure 3.2).

If this heavy, cool air is trapped by a depression at the bottom of the hill, it will pool there and you will have a lens of air that is cooler than the air around it. If this occurs on an evening when the air temperature is near freezing, this lens of cool air can create an area of frost. When this situation arises in an orange grove in the spring, for example, the frost has the potential to freeze the flowers and destroy the year's crop. This problem can be eliminated by creating an artificial wind by using large fans or even by renting a helicopter to fly low overhead and force the air to mix.

This notion of cool air pooling against an obstruction has potential for application in microclimatic design and is used effectively in many hot climates of the world. Air in a courtyard that is completely surrounded by solid walls can be isolated from the prevailing atmosphere and, if cooled by shade trees or fountains, can create a pool of cool air (see Figure 3.3).

A situation known as *advection* can also occur, in which a green area in or near a city can generate air that is cooler than air in the adjacent hard

Figure 3.3 When an area is completely surrounded by a contiguous wall, cool air cannot flow away and will tend to pool. The air temperature in an isolated area like this can be lower than outside the wall.

urban surfaces. Under light wind conditions, this cool air can be pushed horizontally out of the park, acting almost like a natural air cooling system. The effect does not extend far, but, like in the urban heat island situation, lots of green areas can have a cumulative effect and can cool a city in a way similar to how lots of gray areas can warm it.

We looked at the advective effect of paddy fields in Tokyo during a particularly hot period one summer. We carefully measured the air temperature at 1.5 meters (4.9 feet) above a large urban paddy field, then measured the air temperature at 1.5 meters above the ground along neighborhood streets radiating off from the paddy field (see figure 3.4). The air temperature over the paddy field was about 2°C (3.6°F) lower than in the middle of the urban neighborhood. When we moved downwind of the paddy, the temperature gradually rose from the paddy field temperature to

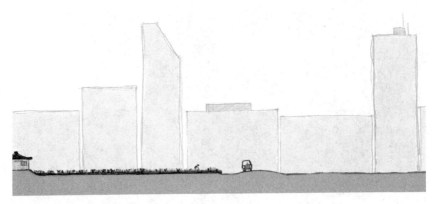

Figure 3.4 Paddy fields in Tokyo create cool green patches. The air above these pad-dies tends to be cooled by evaporation and can be carried by prevailing winds into adjacent neighborhoods.

the urban temperature over a distance of about 150 meters (492 feet). The *boundary layer* set up in a situation like this grows at a rate of about 1 in 100, so the measurements at a height of 1.5 meters would be affected for the first 150 meters from the paddy field. Streets that ran in directions other than downwind of the paddy field received no cooling effect from the paddy field.

So why is our experience so much different than this? A person stand-ing in the parking lot in the full sun would definitely feel as if it was too hot. The person would be receiving a large amount of solar radiation di-rectly from the sun and would also be receiving a large amount of terres-trial radiation from the hot asphalt. Remember, radiation from the sun passes through a clear atmosphere almost as if it weren't even there. Over short distances, the same holds largely true for terrestrial radiation. So the air does not get heated by the radiation. And the air molecules that come in contact with the hot asphalt surface are quickly mixed in with the large number of air molecules nearby and end up having little local effect. Over time, the air temperature will gradually rise, but because of the efficient mixing of the air, it will rise the same amount almost everywhere in the landscape.

HUMIDITY

Tokyo can be almost unbearably hot and humid in the summer. Even though the air temperature might be only a little over 30°C (86°F), it can feel oppressive. In fact, in some ways it feels hotter to me than the 50°C (122°F) temperatures I've experienced in Death Valley, where the air was very dry. This is central to the ongoing debate about hotness, and the impetus for deriving things like the humidity index, or *humidex*. What the humidex tries to do is to combine the effects of air temperature and humidity into a single scale. On a humid day where the actual air temperature is only 25°C (77°F), but the humidex says 35, then it is supposed to *feel* the same as it would on a day when the air temperature is 35°C (95°F) but the humidity is low.

There is no question that humidity in the air affects the thermal comfort of people, but it turns out that the same mechanism that mixes the air molecules so efficiently that we can't find horizontal temperature differences also mixes the water vapor molecules just as efficiently. If you were to walk expeditiously around a landscape measuring humidity in the air at chest height above the ground, you would not be able to find any substantial differences. We say that air temperature and humidity are *horizontally homogeneous* within a landscape at a given point in time.

When water molecules change their state from liquid to vapor, the molecules mix with the dry air molecules and the effect is hardly noticeable until there get to be quite a few vapor molecules in the air. The higher the temperature of the air, the more water it can hold in the form of vapor— and it's not a linear relationship. At 30°C (86°F), the air can hold more than three times as much water vapor as it can at 10°C (50°F). However, the main reason it feels so oppressively hot at times of high humidity is that the opportunity for evaporative cooling from your body and from surfaces is limited. In hot, dry air, perspiration can evaporate freely, carrying heat away from your body with it, but in hot, humid air there is no room for more water vapor in the air, so perspiration isn't able to evaporate.

On that hot, humid day in Tokyo, I ordered a small flask of cold sake to accompany my *nigiri zushi* lunch. In a short time, the flask was completely beaded with wet droplets on the outside. Humidity from the air was condensing on the cool flask. The air *immediately next to* the flask would have a slightly lower humidity than in the prevailing air. Knowing that people sometimes find air with lower humidity to be more comfortable, the process of condensing water out of the air provides an opportunity in microclimatic design.

As in the situation with lowering air temperature, the key is to isolate an area completely from the prevailing atmosphere so that the air doesn't have an opportunity to mix and dissipate the lower-humidity air. A walled garden with some cool surfaces onto which water from the air could condense would lower the humidity in the air. However, condensing water out of the air releases heat to the surface over time, and the surfaces would gradually lose their potential to condense more water from the air. The other issue is a bit more complex and has to do with the molecular weight of water vapor and dry air.

Water vapor molecules are lighter than dry air molecules, so that when a vapor molecule is displaced by a dry air molecule, such as when water is condensed out of the air, the resulting drier air is actually heavier than it was when it was moister. This means that if we are successful in removing humidity from the air, the resulting air will act much as the cooler air did in previous cases and will sink to the ground and stay there unless disturbed. We can ensure that it is not disturbed by having a solid barrier all around it, which keeps out the wind and doesn't allow it to flow out at the base.

Depending on the situation, there are two opportunities to modify air humidity through design. When the air is hot and dry, you can cool the air by adding water and allowing it to evaporate. When the air is hot and humid, you can condense water out of the air, making it drier and more comfortable for people. But in both cases, you have to do this in an isolated environment or the effect will quickly dissipate.

Despite the fact that air temperature and humidity are horizontally homogenous in a landscape, they can both vary greatly with height and time and over large horizontal distances. In the parking lot example, the air temperature immediately next to the sun-drenched asphalt surface would be very high—almost as high as the temperature of the asphalt itself. By the time you reach 1.5 meters (4.9 feet) above the asphalt, the air temperature had fallen 20°C (36°F) to be almost identical to the prevailing air temperature. The graph of this temperature profile looks a lot like the path that a jet would follow if it took off from a runway and then rose as quickly and steeply as possible. The temperature falls off very quickly at first (the path of the jet along the runway and at takeoff) and then changes very little with height as you get farther from the surface (when the jet is going almost straight up). The profile for humidity is similar. Very near a wet surface, the humidity in the air can be very high, but it falls off precipitously a short distance away.

There is also a variation in air temperature and humidity with time. Generally, the coolest time of the day is just before sunrise as the earth and the air have had all night to cool down without the input of solar radiation. Then the earth heats up as it absorbs solar radiation, reaching a maximum near midday, but the air temperature, because it is heated from below through contact with the earth, reaches its maximum a little later in the day. The maximum air temperature normally occurs in the early to mid-afternoon.

And, of course, there are tremendous variations in air temperature and humidity on a global scale. Temperatures as low as −89.2°C (−128.6°F) have been recorded in Antarctica, and temperatures as high as 57.8°C (136°F) have been documented in Libya. Humidity at various places on earth at any time ranges from near 0 percent to 100 percent.

The amount of humidity in the air can be measured in a number of different ways, some of which are more accurate and precise than others. Many of the measurements are based on the concept of a wet sock. You might have had the experience as a kid of getting a soaker—when you stepped into a puddle that was deeper than you expected or your foot slid off the shore and into the edge of a river or lake. Your sock and shoe got soaked. If this has happened to you, you likely will also have experienced the chill that often accompanies a soaker. The water might have been cold, but even if it wasn't, over time your foot would likely have gotten cooler and cooler. As the water in your sock evaporated, it would have taken heat from your foot.

Now consider taking a regular mercury-in-glass thermometer and putting a wet sock onto the bulb. As the water evaporates from the sock, it will take heat from the thermometer, resulting in a reading that is lower than air temperature. It is this difference between the wet-bulb and the dry-bulb temperatures that yields a measure of the humidity in the air. When the air has a high amount of humidity in it, little water will be able to evaporate from the sock and the temperature difference will be small. But when the air is very dry, a lot of water will evaporate from the sock, taking a lot of heat from the wet-bulb thermometer and creating a big difference in the temperature of the two thermometers. In order for this system to work well, both the wet-bulb and the dry-bulb thermometers need to be shielded from radiation and to have a wind pass over them. This can be accomplished by using a fan, or the instruments can be spun around in the air. The dorkiest but still effective microclimate instrument ever invented is the *sling psychrometer*. You have to spin the instrument in a horizontal circle over your head or in front of you for at least a minute or two and then quickly take the readings from the two thermometers. Then you can use a simple graph to determine the humidity level in the air.

We should discuss one more point about humidity here. Weather forecasts tend to report on something called *relative humidity*. This is a ratio of the amount of humidity in the air relative to the maximum amount that the air will hold. But there's a catch. The maximum amount of water vapor that the air can hold *changes with temperature,* and it isn't a linear relationship. So if you hear that the relative humidity has fallen, you don't know whether it is because there is less humidity in the air or because the temperature of the air has risen and the maximum amount of moisture that the air can hold has also risen.

This can lead to some very confusing situations. I was watching an Olympic marathon on television once, and the announcers were discussing how hot and humid it was for the runners. They reported that at eight o'clock in the morning the air temperature was already 30°C (86°F) and the humidity was 84 percent. They continued to comment on the weather and the fact that the air temperature continued to rise through the race, but they were surprised to see that the relative humidity went down over time. They said something like, "The conditions have improved a bit for the runners. Despite the air temperature rising to 33°C (91.4°F), the relative humidity has actually fallen off a bit to only 78 percent." Well, certainly the conditions for the runners were not better as the day wore on. There was essentially the same amount of water vapor in the air, probably a bit more actually as water evaporated from the vegetation along the marathon route. But because they were reporting *relative* humidity, as the air temperature rose the relative humidity value went down. Everyone, including sports announcers, would be better off if we talked about *absolute humidity* in the air.

SOLAR RADIATION

The earth is almost twelve thousand kilometers (7,450 miles) in diameter, yet most of our atmosphere—about 80 percent—is within fifteen kilometers (9 miles) of the surface. Now, a fifteen-kilometer-thick layer might seem like a lot of air when you are looking up at it from your position down here at the bottom, but if you were to scale the earth down to something the size of, say, a basketball, the atmosphere would be less than one millimeter thick. If you included virtually all of the atmosphere, it would still only be a layer two millimeters thick. You would be hard pressed to spread peanut butter in a layer that thin on a basketball.

So, earth is basically a ball floating in space with a very thin layer of atmosphere attached to it. As we all memorized at one time or another in our lives, the earth revolves around the sun at an average distance of about 150 million kilometers (93 million miles). But the important fact that you might not have learned, or may have long forgotten, is that as the earth revolves around the sun it is *tilted*. Now, it's a bit difficult to try to imagine how something floating in space is tilted. After all, there is no up or down in space. But *relative to the sun*, the earth is tilted at about 23 degrees. It's actually closer to 23.4 degrees, but when trying to remember what the value is, I like to think of it as being *about* half of 45 degrees, which is half of 90 degrees, which is half of 180 degrees, which is half of 360 degrees, a full circle. In any event, this tilt is pretty important for a whole variety of reasons, but the most important for this discussion is that it means that for half the year we are tilted toward the sun and for the other half we are tilted away.

Wherever you live on earth, the time that your home is tilted toward the sun will be summer and the time when you are tilted away will be winter. Try this. Make a fist with your right hand, and point your thumb straight up. Now rotate your wrist until your thumb is pointing toward the left wall. Then move your thumb until it is halfway between pointing at the wall and at the ceiling—this will be about half of 90 degrees, or 45 degrees. Then go halfway from that point to the ceiling, and your fist will be tilted at about 22.5 degrees, about the same tilt as the earth. Now move your hand to a position to the immediate right of this book (which you are now balancing precariously on your knees), and imagine that the book is the sun. You will see that the knuckle of your pointer finger will now be facing toward the sun and would be experiencing summertime sunshine. The knuckle of your pinky finger, in the meantime, would be tilted away from the sun and would be in midwinter.

Now, keeping your thumb pointed at the same angle, tilted 22.5 degrees from vertical, move your hand to the left of the book. Now the knuckle of your pointer finger will be pointed away from the sun and it would be wintertime. Your pinky is now tilted toward the sun and it would be summer there.

Of course, there is much more to it than this. To simulate the movement of the earth over time, you would have to be able to spin your fist around your thumb and move your fist in circles around the book. But in general, it gives a reasonable representation of the relative positions of the earth and the sun.

So now that you have had to contort yourself, what is the point? Well, it all comes down to *intensity* of radiation—that is, the amount of solar radiation per unit area. The same amount of radiation can be spread over a large area when the sun is lower in the sky (low intensity) and over a much smaller area when the sun is higher in the sky (high intensity). If you could see the radiation being emitted by your book (remember, it will be emitting terrestrial radiation, which is invisible to the human eye), the part of your hand tilted *toward* the book would be receiving a higher *intensity* of radiation than the part tilted away.

This concept is probably still a bit fuzzy. No worries. Let's try something else that might make it clearer. Take three identical, black, rectilinear objects, something like black notebooks. On a sunny day, set one in the sun so that the largest face of it (the front of the book) is perpendicular to the sun—that is, the sun is falling directly onto it and it has the highest intensity of solar radiation possible. Orient a second one so that the sun's rays are parallel to the largest face so that almost no direct solar radiation is falling on the object and the intensity of solar radiation is very low. Put the third in an intermediate position, at an angle halfway between the first two. Make sure that there is little or no wind passing over the books, and then, after a few minutes in the sun, put your hand on each of the three objects in turn and check their temperatures. The object perpendicular to the sun, which is receiving the highest intensity of radiation, will be the warmest object, and the one parallel to the sun's rays will be the coolest.

You can check out the intensity of radiation on a global scale if you ever travel a considerable distance to the north or south within a short time period. I had an opportunity one June to travel to three locations separated by about 10 degrees of latitude within a week—Atlanta, Georgia, at about 34 degrees N; Guelph, Ontario, at about 44 degrees N; and Sturgeon Landing, Saskatchewan, at about 54 degrees N (see figure 3.5).

In Atlanta, the sun was so high at noon that I hardly cast a shadow. The intensity of radiation on horizontal surfaces was about as high as it could possibly be. In Guelph, my shadow at noon was longer than in Atlanta and the intensity of the radiation on horizontal surfaces was lower (that is, the

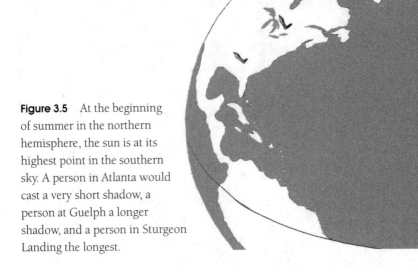

Figure 3.5   At the beginning of summer in the northern hemisphere, the sun is at its highest point in the southern sky. A person in Atlanta would cast a very short shadow, a person at Guelph a longer shadow, and a person in Sturgeon Landing the longest.

radiation had to be spread over a larger area). Finally, in Sturgeon Landing, my shadow was quite long and the intensity of radiation on horizontal surfaces was quite a bit lower than in Guelph.

Here's another experiment that you can do at home. It isn't difficult, but it takes a bit of time and dedication. Put five stakes in the ground in the pattern of an X—one stake where the two arms cross, and one at the end of each arm, with each arm of the cross pointing to a main compass direction (north, east, south, and west). Then, over the period of a year, observe where the sun rises and sets relative to the four directions and notice how long the shadows of the stakes are at different times of the year. You'll find that the sun rises due east and sets due west only on the equinoxes in March and September, and that in the winter the sun rises in the southeast and sets in the southwest (your latitude will determine how far toward the south). In summer, it will rise in the northeast and set in the northwest. You will see that the shadows of the stakes are longest in winter and shortest in summer.

This is invaluable information for use in microclimatic design. It illustrates how the position and movement of the sun changes through the seasons. The position and movement also changes as a function of your position on the planet. During my trip to Atlanta, I observed that the sun came up in the east-northeast, was very high in the sky at noon, and set in the west-northwest. In Guelph, the sun came up in the northeast, was quite high in the sky at noon, and set in the northwest. And in Sturgeon Landing, the sun rose in the north-northeast, was not very high in the sky at noon, and set in the north-north west. Even the middle of the night wasn't very dark, as the sun seemed to be passing just below the horizon.

So, there were big differences in the three places. The most surprising thing for most people is to discover that the sun doesn't always rise in the east and set in the west. The most that could be said is that the sun rises in the eastern sky and sets in the western sky, but certainly it is seldom due east and due west.

Here's one more experiment to try on a sunny day. Take three of your tee shirts, one that's black, one that's white, and one of an intermediate color. Lay them out side by side on a dry surface, such as a board or a picnic table, in the full sun and away from any wind. Angle them so that the intensity of the solar radiation falling on them is high, and wait a few minutes. Then put your hand on each one in turn and test its temperature. The black one will be the hottest because most of the solar radiation falling on this shirt will be absorbed into the material. The white shirt will be the coolest since most of the solar radiation falling on it is reflected away. The intermediate shirt will have an intermediate temperature. This will undoubtedly give you some good ideas of what to wear on hot sunny days, but it should also make you consider that the color of materials that you put in a landscape will have a major impact on their temperature and, as a consequence, on the microclimate around them.

These simple experiments demonstrate three of the most powerful and useful microclimate modification principles. By understanding how the sun moves through the sky during different times of the year and then simply changing the color of a material or its orientation relative to the sun, you can substantially affect surface temperatures and, consequently, the microclimate.

Let's consider what is happening. All of the solar radiation arriving at a surface must go somewhere, since energy can be neither created nor destroyed. The amount of radiation per unit area, the *intensity* of the radiation, is a function of the orientation of an object relative to the sun. As we saw in our experiment, the more nearly perpendicular the object is to the sun, the higher the intensity of radiation received.

The radiation that is received at the surface must be either reflected or absorbed. The amount that is absorbed by an object is a function of its color. Darker colors absorb more solar radiation than lighter colors. The ability of an object to reflect solar radiation is known as its *albedo*. In our experiment, the white tee shirt had a high albedo, while the black one had a low albedo.

If we could see, in slow motion, solar radiation moving through the landscape, it would be a bit like a jet of water in a world of sponges of various densities (see figure 3.6). When a jet of water hits a very porous sponge (like solar radiation striking a dark surface), most of the water is absorbed into the sponge and little is deflected away. If that same jet, however, were to hit a solid, impermeable, smooth-surfaced sponge (like solar radiation striking a light-colored surface), very little of the water will be absorbed and most will be deflected onto other surfaces. It will bounce around from surface to surface until it is absorbed or deflected out of the space (in this analogy, you have to imagine that the water doesn't slow down when it hits surfaces).

Here's another oddity about the sun that you might not have noticed. The sun moves faster through the sky in summer than it does in winter. Now, there are some who will tell you that the sun doesn't actually *move* but that, rather, it is the earth moving around the sun that makes it *appear* that the sun is moving. They are not wrong. However, because of relativity, it is also not wrong to say that the sun moves through the sky. In fact, no

Figure 3.6 If our eyes could see solar radiation moving, in slow motion, through the landscape, it would look similar to a stream of water being sprayed against a surface. Some of the water would be absorbed by the surface, and some would be deflected away.

one can prove you wrong (and some pretty great minds have tried) if you were to say that everything in the universe revolves around *you!*

Back to the speed of the sun moving through the sky. If you timed how long it took the sun to move from southeast to south in June in New York, you would find that it takes about one hour. In January at the same location the sun takes about three hours to move the same number of degrees. This has important implications in terms of capturing sun in winter and repelling it in summer.

Now, how do we measure the amount of solar radiation in different parts of the landscape? Many different instruments have been designed to measure this visible and invisible energy, but only a few are of any particular value in microclimatic landscape design. Let me start by telling you some of the instruments that you should not use—ever.

First of all, you shouldn't ever use a light meter to measure solar radiation. Remember that only about half of the radiation from the sun can be seen, while the other half is invisible to human eyes. We still *feel the heat* of the invisible portion in the same way as we feel the visible portion, so it has to be considered in any energy budget—but light meters don't sense it so will give faulty readings. There's another twist to the story too. Trees have adapted to use only part of the visible portion of the solar spectrum to grow. Their leaves allow much of the invisible portion, known as *solar infrared radiation*, to pass through. So, when you sit under a tree it might look quite shady to your eyes, but in fact there can be a fairly large amount of solar infrared radiation from the sun washing over your body. If, instead, you sat in the shade of a solid structure such as a building, there would be far less solar infrared radiation washing over you because it would be intercepted by the building. Even though the shade of a tree and the shade of a building might look quite similar to your eye, there is a lot more solar radiation passing through the tree while none is passing through a solid building. A person under a tree would have a higher input of energy than someone in the shade of a building. So, your eyes can play tricks on you. What you see is not necessarily what you get.

So far we have been talking about solar radiation that comes directly from the sun and arrives at a surface, but not all of it makes it through the atmosphere unchanged. The sizes of air molecules are exactly the right size to deflect the blue wavelengths. When you look up and see a blue sky, what you are looking at are the blue wavelengths of solar radiation that are being scattered about in the atmosphere like pool balls on a crowded billiard table. Besides adding a colorful dimension to our landscapes (the "sky" on the moon, for example, has no color), it also adds radiation to shaded areas. You might have thought that the shade of a building would have absolutely no solar radiation in it, since the building is solid. However, the solar radiation deflected by air molecules, often called *sky radiation* or *diffuse radiation*, adds energy to the landscape the same as any other radiation. On a clear day, the amount of solar radiation in the shade of a solid structure will be about 10 percent of what it is in the open, and on cloudy days there can be nearly as much solar radiation in the shade of a building as there is in the open.

We've already discussed how some of the solar infrared radiation passes through leaves of trees. Add to that some diffuse radiation scattered from the sky, and it is starting to look like trees don't provide nearly as much shade as you might think.

So, how *should* solar radiation be measured? The most effective way is through the use of an instrument called a *pyranometer*. In full sun on a clear day, the reading from an instrument like this would be around 1000 watts per square meter (W/m²). Hourly readings with instruments like this are often taken at a few key locations, such as airports in major cities. The instrument is set on a horizontal surface in the middle of a flat grassed area that has been mown quite short—to make sure that the landscape is not affecting the reading in any way.

TERRESTRIAL RADIATION

A few years ago, I was teaching an urban design course in London, England, and had decided to take a weekend trip to Dublin, Ireland, to visit a former graduate student who was practicing landscape architecture there. The train ride had been fine, but the ferry had not been very warm and the wind off the sea had penetrated my thin jacket and chilled me to the core. Once on land, we transferred off the ferry and walked to the train, and— although we were still outdoors—I suddenly felt quite warm. I became aware that there were some radiation heaters along the walkway (similar to the catalytic heater that we used to survive the cold of the football game). As at the football game, this heater was not heating the air but simply bathing us in an invisible stream of terrestrial radiation.

Every space in the landscape and every part of a microclimate are full of terrestrial radiation, and it is impossible to see any of it with the human eye. There are instruments that will *see* and measure this radiation, but fortunately there is also a very simple relationship between the temperature of an object and the amount of radiation that it emits. You might not think it is fortunate when I first tell you what the formula is, but since the advent of calculators and computers, the equation has gone from a lion to a pussycat. Here is what it says: take the temperature of the object in Celsius (T), add

273 to convert it to Kelvins (K), take the result to the power four, and then multiply the answer by 5.67×10^{-8} (which basically means 0.0000000567; a constant known as sigma [σ]), and the answer will be the amount of terrestrial radiation (R) emitted by the object. Here is how it looks written out:

$$R = \sigma \times K^4$$

Simply plug that formula into your computer or calculator, and then if you ever want to know how much energy is being emitted by an object, put in the temperature and out will pop the answer. We know from our earlier discussion that when I was slothing on the couch I was generating about 60 W/m² of internal energy. How much energy do you think that I was emitting? Let's assume that my skin was at about 33°C (91.4°F) and the formula would say that we add 273 to 33 to get 306 Kelvins. Take this to the fourth power and multiply it by σ and we get 497 W/m². Yikes! Where is all that energy coming from? Am I really emitting that much radiation?

For comparison, let's check how much energy I would be getting from the walls and objects in the room. They are probably at about 20°C (68°F), so using our formula we would calculate that I would be receiving 415 W/m². So the difference, or *net terrestrial radiation*, is about 497 – 415 = 82 W/m². My body is emitting 82 W/m² more than it is receiving. That sounds more reasonable. And this might make me feel a bit cool if I didn't have many clothes on, but if I had on a shirt and pants, then the surface of my clothing would likely be much lower than 33°C (91.4°F), probably more like 25°C (77°F). If this were the case, then we could again use our formula to see that I would be emitting 447 W/m². My terrestrial radiation balance would be 447 going out and 415 coming in, for a net terrestrial radiation budget of 32 W/m² away from my body—an amount that would be hardly noticeable.

So the real key is not the *absolute* amount of terrestrial radiation you are receiving from an object but, rather, the amount *relative* to the amount

on. This is an instrument that every landscape architect should
doing a site visit—to allow the person to "see" the hot and cold
he landscape.

ually start by pointing it at the walls and see that they are the
erature as the air in the room—about 20°C (68°F). This trans-
about 418 W/m² that is being emitted by the walls. We then
temperature of a person's clothing and usually find that it is
e around 22°C (71.6°F), which means that they are emitting
W/m². This translates into a net radiation budget of about 11
very small exchange of energy. After checking temperatures of
g interesting in the classroom and finding only very small differ-
head outside. Suddenly, the invisible streams of radiation in the
e are made visible through the radiation thermometer. On a typi-
y, when the air temperature is about 15°C (59°F), the range of ter-
diation emitted by different surfaces in the landscape can be quite
lar. Asphalt surfaces, because the black surface is absorbing a lot of
radiation it receives, can be emitting more than 500 W/m², while
walls in the shade can be emitting less than 350. The net terres-
iation for the person whose clothing was at 22°C (71.6°F) would
t +70 W/m² if near the asphalt surface and –80 W/m² if near the
e. These differences are not huge when compared with the amount
radiation that can be received, but they can tip the balance in favor
g thermally comfortable rather than too warm or too cool.

ce the students are starting to feel comfortable with the idea of
s of radiation that relate to the temperatures of objects, someone in-
y points the radiation thermometer at the sky—and causes quite a
otion.

ow, normally, the field study components of my courses are held no
r what the conditions of the day. The topic of microclimate is the one
tion. While soils don't change much from day to day or as a result of
eather, the microclimate does. If you go looking for microclimates on
y, calm days, you will find that the differences are minimized. But dif-
ces in microclimates are maximized on sunny, windy days. So when a

that you are emitting. If the balance is g
are receiving a lot more than you are emi
you feel warmer. If the balance is the ot
of terrestrial radiation and will feel cool
environments is to be strategic with the
doesn't normally have the same level of ii
on your thermal comfort. But there are c
strongly influence a person's thermal comf

You might have had an opportunity to
ing. That fire would have been a major sou
air that was heated by the fire rose quick
air above, but the terrestrial radiation woul
energy that warmed you. If it was a cool eve
enced the condition of the front of your bod
restrial radiation load from the fire while the
cool due to the small amount of terrestrial rac
cold landscape.

My apartment in Tokyo was on a street tl
playground for wealthy young Japanese, and t
to cater to their every desire. One of their desi
and be seen." Even on winter days (which are g
cold in Tokyo), people wanted to sit long into th
along the street. The businesses with radiant h
among the tables were the most popular by far.
heaters even though they couldn't see the strear
that was bathing them. Microclimate modification
positive economic consequence for the proprietors

If you want to "see" terrestrial radiation, ther
that will assist you. There are devices with special fil
restrial radiation to enter the instrument. The senso
ing of the amount of terrestrial radiation being rece
calculate the temperature of the object that emitted
use a *radiation thermometer* in my classes to help stuc

trial radiati
have when
places in th
We us
same temp
lates into
check the
somewhe
about 42
W/m^2, a
everythir
ences, w
landscap
cal fall d
restrial r
spectacu
the sola
concret
trial rac
be abou
concret
of solai
of beir
O
stream
evitab
comm

N
matte
excep
the v
clouc
feren

student points the radiation thermometer at the sky, it is always a clear sky in the middle of the day. And the amount of radiation being emitted from the sky is only a little over 200 W/m^2, suggesting that the temperature of the sky is about −20°C (−4°F)! The students are emitting over 400 W/m^2 and receiving only 200 W/m^2 from the sky, resulting in a large net loss of terrestrial radiation to the sky.

Think about the implications of this deficit in terms of the landscape. During the day, the effect tends to be minimal compared to the large input of solar radiation, but shut off the solar input at sunset and all of a sudden this terrestrial radiation deficit can become pretty important. Consider a warm spring day when the apple trees on the hillsides are in full bloom. The sunny day becomes a clear evening, and the stars burst out of the sky. Invisible to our eye, the hilltop above the apple trees is emitting lots of terrestrial radiation upward but is receiving much less back from the sky. At first the effect is minimal, but over time the ground cools down, eventually becoming very cool. The air that touches the ground gets cooled as well, and with it being a calm evening there is no wind to mix the cool air. A bubble of cool air forms on top of the hill and begins to slide down the hill like syrup flowing off pancakes. In the middle of the slope, the apple trees are fine because as the cool air passes it draws some warm air from above in its wake, but at the bottom of the slope it's a different story. If the air has nowhere to go when it reaches the bottom—say, if there is a depression with no outlet or if there is a windbreak blocking the air from flowing farther—the cool air will accumulate. And if it gets cold enough, the blossoms on the apple trees at the bottom of the slope will freeze.

Why doesn't this happen every evening? First of all, if there are clouds in the sky, they emit terrestrial radiation at a much higher level than a clear sky does, so the ground and the clouds can reach an equilibrium and very little cooling of the ground will take place. This is the main reason it is often relatively warm on mornings after a cloudy night. Second, if there are trees on the hilltop, it will be the tops of the trees that will exchange terrestrial radiation with the sky and that can become quite frosty on clear evenings. The terrestrial radiation emitted by the ground will be received by the tree canopy, and the tree canopy will emit terrestrial radiation to the ground, resulting in an equilibrium; consequently, the ground under the tree will not cool down as much as ground open to the sky. This relationship explains something that you often see after the first few frosts in the fall—white frost on the grass but green frostless grass under trees.

These principles can be applied very easily to the design of outdoor environments. On cool evenings, people will find it to be more thermally comfortable under the canopy of a tree, or under an umbrella or a trellis, than out in the open. If the air is cool, then people will also appreciate warm surfaces under and beside them that will bathe them in terrestrial radiation. They won't be able to see it, nor will most of them understand why it is more comfortable, but they will appreciate it nonetheless.

To give a sense of the importance of terrestrial radiation in human thermal comfort, the other day my colleague phoned me from down the hall and said, "I was comfortable in my office yesterday, but today I'm feeling quite chilly. I haven't adjusted my thermostat, so what's going on Dr. Thermal Comfort?" (a nickname I don't really relish). I said, "Don't move. . . . I'll be right there." I grabbed my radiation thermometer and when I got to his office I saw that he was sitting at his desk facing a large window. I measured the amount of terrestrial radiation being emitted by the window (it was 13°C [55°F] so was emitting approximately 379 W/m^2), and the amount being emitted by his face (32°C [90°F], so 491W/m^2), which indicated a deficit of more than 100 W/m^2. As he sat facing the window, he was emitting more terrestrial radiation than he was receiving, and over time it was making him chilly. The previous day had been much warmer outside, and the temperature of his window would also have been warmer—resulting in less of a radiation imbalance.

WIND

The tilt of the earth relative to the sun means that areas near the equator receive the highest intensity of solar radiation while areas near the two poles receive the lowest. This sets up a simple but very grand scale system in the atmosphere in which the air near the equator is relatively warm while the air near the poles is relatively cool. These two regions of air mix about as well as oil and water, and the interface between the two air masses has become known as a *front*. The term *front* was introduced by Jacob Bjerknes, a Norwegian who had the idea that masses of air of different temperatures bumped up against each other like a couple of World War I armies. The analogy is not a bad one and is the concept at the theoretical heart of meteorology today. It is like a long, ongoing war where neither side really makes much progress, and if they do move forward for a while, they end up losing ground later.

If, at the very coarse scale, you were to draw a picture of the earth and the atmosphere, the cool air would sit like a toque on the top and bottom of the globe. The rest of the atmosphere would be the warm air. These toques expand and shrink with the seasons, with the toque on the north getting larger during winter and smaller during summer. Think of it as pulling your toque down over your ears in winter but letting it sit on top of your head like a Rasta in summer. The location of the global front between the cold and warm air masses is controlled by the size of the toque. In winter the front moves toward the equator, while in summer it recedes toward the pole.

Unfortunately, we now have to complicate this picture slightly by taking into consideration that the earth is spinning around underneath the atmosphere. And it's not exactly a slow and lazy spin. At the equator, the earth is spinning at more than 1,600 kilometers (994 miles) per hour, and even around London, in the middle latitudes where the fronts hang around, the speed is still close to 1,000 kilometers (621 miles) per hour. The atmosphere is in contact with, but not attached to, the earth, so the movement of the earth drags the bottom of the atmosphere along, making the whole atmosphere rotate slowly in the same direction as the earth— that is, from west to east. So, with the atmosphere being dragged from below by the earth, the result is that in general winds blow from the westerly directions in the middle latitudes. This sets the whole system in motion and sets up a wave along the front between the warm and cool air. These waves are responsible for the weather systems that we know as cold and warm fronts.

Along with these systems are areas known as low-pressure systems and high-pressure systems. The air responds to these pressure differences by flowing from the areas of higher pressure to those of lower pressure, but because of the spin of the earth, the air can't move in a straight line but, rather, arcs out from areas of high pressure and arcs into areas of low pressure. It's one of the weird consequences of living with Cartesian coordinates (straight lines, flat surfaces, and so forth) in a rotating spherical world. Most of the things we do and the things we measure are much more easily done in Cartesian coordinates so, rather than changing our whole system of coordinates and calculations, in 1835 a fellow named Gaspard-Gustave de Coriolis had a brilliant idea: he suggested that we add an *imaginary* force to our calculations about air movement in the atmosphere to take into account the movement of the earth. The *coriolis force* was born and started to be used in meteorology in the early 1900s, and it is still in use today.

The consequence for those of us stuck to the surface of the earth and spinning with it is that we experience a lot of winds that flow from west to east, and since we have a convention of naming winds from whence they blow, it is common to have a *prevailing westerly wind* in midlatitude regions of the world. The wind won't be westerly all the time because every time a frontal system passes, the wind will blow from each direction of the compass for at least a few minutes or hours and then will typically settle back into a westerly flow.

As I was growing up on the Canadian prairies, wind was my constant, usually unwelcome, companion: hot dry winds in summer, cold penetrating winds in winter. The wind always seemed to be blowing from out of the west. When I was on adventures with my buddies, we were always on the lookout for places in the landscape where we could escape from the wind. One place where we found them was in the *coulees*, a local term for small valleys. We could get out of the wind and drop out of sight at the same time.

We knew that the windiest place was on the windward crest of the hill. Here we could lean far into the wind and not fall over. The wind was the calmest on the lee side of the hill near the base, and we found that vegetation slowed it even more. Even on the windiest of days, we could find a spot that was sheltered from the wind where we could light a campfire and relax. I learned that landforms can direct and deflect the wind, as do trees and shrubs. In an environment where the winds were so constantly and predictably from the west, we could rely on the east side of a chokecherry grove on the eastern base of a hill to be calm most of the time. Other characteristics of the wind were less predictable and understandable.

One of my first jobs was as a hired hand for a fellow named Bernie. His ranch in the Great Sandhills of Saskatchewan provided me a lot of opportunities to experience the wind. It was virtually treeless, and the wind carried away anything that wasn't tied down. Bernie had built some rough-looking fences, with lots of missing boards, right beside the place where he put out winter feed for his cattle.

The fences were oriented in a north-south direction so as to provide a windbreak from the prevailing westerly winds. One day I asked Bernie why he didn't replace the missing boards (see figure 3.7). He explained that the fence made a better windbreak the way it was. A solid fence would create a lot of turbulence and only a very small area right next to it where the wind would be very slow. Not many cattle could fit into that small space. The staggered-board fence created a much larger area of reduced wind that allowed a lot of cattle to benefit from it. It's the same situation with the snow fences along the roads. They are also about 50 percent porous, which seems to be the most efficient for catching drifting snow before it reaches the roads.

The porosity of a windbreak is a very important determinant of its effectiveness. Many studies have demonstrated that the optimum porosity

Figure 3.7 Cattle fences on the Canadian prairies are often constructed of rough-cut lumber that leaves lots of spaces for air to pass through. This amount of porosity provides a more effective windbreak than a solid fence with no gaps.

is somewhere near 50 percent, just as Bernie had learned through trial and error. If a windbreak is too dense, it will create only a small area of low wind speed, while a barrier that is too porous creates a large area with barely discernible wind reduction. The way to achieve this desired porosity ranges from wooden fences to various species of plants. The Eastern white cedar has a nearly ideal porosity when grown on sixty-centimeter (twenty-four-inch) centers.

Windbreaks are most effective when oriented perpendicular to the wind, but with the wind constantly changing directions, it is impossible to have an ideal windbreak without completely surrounding an area. Which leads us to the last big question in microclimatology: how to describe the way the wind moves in and around elements in the landscape. Solve this one, and I'll nominate you for a Nobel Prize in classical physics. We simply don't have equations or computer models powerful enough to accurately and precisely predict wind flow in complex environments, although some commercially available software is getting close through the use of numerical simulations.

In the meantime, we have to rely on physical simulations and general patterns. Simulations are done by building scale models of the landscape and inserting them into a wind tunnel. You then turn on the fan, forcing air to flow over your model, and you measure the relative speeds of the wind in various locations in your model landscape. You can then insert scale models of windbreaks or buildings and see what effect they have under various wind conditions. It is a bit time-consuming and expensive, but it is currently the best way to predict the way your landscape will interact with the wind. The advantage of using a wind tunnel is that, if you get it wrong the first time, it is fairly easy to change the model and test again, whereas if you have already built the landscape it can be very expensive to change.

There are ways to increase the wind speed somewhat, but not nearly as dramatically as wind speeds can be reduced. Winds can be slowed to nearly a standstill, but only naturally increased by maybe 20 percent or so.

Using a wind tunnel can sometimes be impractical or too costly, and in those situations you can often rely on patterns that have been observed and recorded. For example, it is well understood that wind speed increases with distance above the ground, and decreases when it travels over rough surfaces. Wind will flow only if it has somewhere to go. If there is an opening on the windward side of a house, little air will flow in unless there is also an opening somewhere else that allows it to flow out. Wind approaching a hill will be forced to compress slightly and speed up, and then on the lee side of the hill the air will decompress and slow down. As wind approaches a windbreak or structure in the landscape, it will flow over and around it, but if the structure is not very permeable there will be a low-pressure area set up on the lee side. This low pressure will draw air in, creating a turbulent environment. If the structure is somewhat permeable, then a small amount of air will be able to pass through and break up the low-pressure area. Wind will not be drawn in, and turbulence will be reduced. Smooth, streamlined objects will tend to allow the wind to pass easily over and around them, while rectilinear objects will create turbulence and complex wind patterns. Tall buildings can intercept fast-moving

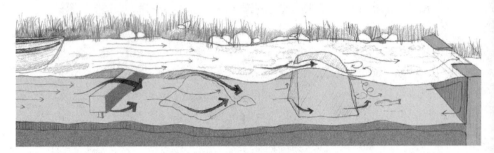

Figure 3.8 Air moving through a landscape is invisible, but it moves in ways very similar to the movement of water in a channel. Turbulent eddies form behind rectilinear structures, and air flows over and around more streamlined objects.

air high above the surface and can force it down toward the ground. This can create very high speed and turbulent winds in urban areas. Because the wind is essentially invisible to us, unless it is carrying snowflakes or dust, it can be valuable to visualize it as being analogous to the movement of another fluid: water in a stream (see figure 3.8).

The speed of the wind and the temperature difference between a person and the air are the two most important determinants of the amount of convection (usually cooling) that will take place. When there is a large difference in temperature, such as a person's skin exposed to winter winds, the amount of heat carried away by convection is high, while in summer, when the air temperature can be very nearly the same as a person's skin temperature, the amount of heat carried away by convection is very low. In fact, if the air is the same temperature as a person's skin, then no heat is carried away, and if the air temperature is higher than a person's skin temperature, then it can actually add heat to the person, making him or her warmer. You can test this yourself if you ever go into a sauna. The air temperature will be higher than your skin temperature. Create a wind by blowing onto your forearm. The wind will feel hot, an indication that the convection was carrying heat *to* your arm. This certainly demonstrated why the wind is so much more effective in cooling people in cold weather than in warm or hot weather.

The goal for the thermal comfort of people, then, is generally to decrease wind speeds in cold seasons and to increase them, if possible, in warm weather. Even in very hot conditions, people like to have some air movement.

The first problem to consider, as we have already discussed, is that the wind does not blow consistently from any one direction. In fact, on any given day, it can blow from any and every direction. This makes if difficult to block without creating a windbreak on all sides. However, the wind will tend to blow from a predominant direction in each different region and in each different season. These patterns are available from published data. For example, about 60 percent of winds in Halifax, Nova Scotia, during the winter are from the west, northwest, and north, while 60 percent in the summer are from the south, southwest, and west.

Wind data can be graphically represented by a *wind rose*. This handy diagram is a series of lines drawn out from a small circle in the middle, with one line for each direction of the compass. Figure 3.9 shows a wind rose for Halifax in winter and summer. The length of the line indicates the percentage of time that the wind typically blows from each direction. A wind rose can readily indicate if there were any prevailing winds—that is, directions from which the wind blows more often than from others.

The speed and direction of the wind are generally measured at ten meters (thirty-three feet) above a level, well-mown grassed surface with no obstructions or vegetation for quite a distance in all directions. One of the few places that typically meet these criteria are airports, so climate stations are often established on or near major airports. *Anemometers* are typically used to measure wind speed. The most common of these is called a *cup anemometer*, as it has three cups that look like ping-pong balls cut in half mounted on a stand. The cups catch the wind and make the instrument spin; the faster it spins, the higher the wind speed. This instrument works quite well in unobstructed situations like an airport but is of limited value in a complex environment where turbulence invalidates the reading.

Many other types of instruments have also been devised, including one called a *hot-wire anemometer*, which consists of a tiny wire that is kept at a

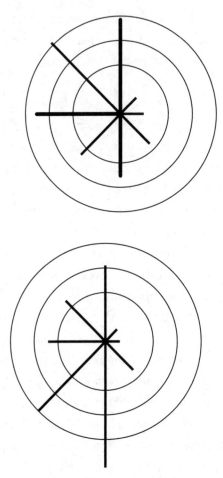

Figure 3.9 These two wind roses show the percentage of the time during (a) winter and (b) summer that the wind blows from each direction. Note that in winter the winds blow predominantly from the west, northwest, and north, but in summer the winds blow more typically from the south and southwest.

constant temperature. As the wind cools it, the amount of energy needed to keep it at a constant temperature yields a measure of the wind speed. However, all it takes is for one bird to decide to land on it, or one spider who decides to built a web on it, and the instrument quits working. It's not very robust and mostly is reserved for scientific study.

Wind direction is usually measured through the use of a simple vane. This is simply a paddle of some sort mounted on a spindle; when it catches the wind, it turns so that the wind passes by without obstruction. The direction is recorded, but if you ever have a chance to watch a wind vane on a breezy day, you will notice that there is a lot of variation in the direction of wind flow—*a lot*! Sometimes the wind can blow from virtually every direction within a minute or two. In order to make some sense of this, an average wind direction over an hour is sometimes calculated, or sometimes the direction that the wind blew from the most during the hour is recorded. Either way, it is a generalization, and it's important to remember that there can be a lot of variation in the data. It's also important to remember that the data recorded at a weather station give an indication of conditions prevailing in an area but will not be exactly the same as the conditions at a landscape some distance from the weather station.

PRECIPITATION

Some mechanisms that we have already discussed can help to explain how and why precipitation occurs. Some of the solar radiation that is absorbed by the ground surface evaporates available water to create vapor, and some of it heats the ground, which in turn heats the air that comes in contact with it. This warmed air will rise, and as it rises it cools. Cooler air cannot hold as much humidity as warmer air, so at some point in its cooling, air will become completely saturated, holding as much water as it is possible for it to hold. If it continues to rise and cools further, then it has to get rid of some of the water vapor that it has in it. It does this by condensing the vapor back into liquid water.

In general, these condensed water particles are initially very small. However, they soon start to collide with one another and start to coalesce into water droplets. When these droplets are heavy enough that the air can no longer hold them up, they will fall to the earth as precipitation. When there are strong updrafts of wind, these particles can grow quite large before they fall. The temperature near the ground will determine whether we experience the precipitation as rain, snow, sleet, or hail.

Air can also be forced to rise by coming in contact with topography. For example, the Cypress Hills in southwestern Saskatchewan, which we discussed earlier, were originally known as the Thunder Hills. Air masses moving across the prairies are forced by elevation change to rise, thus cooling the air and causing condensation and precipitation, which is often accompanied by lightning and thunder.

Precipitation is fairly challenging to measure mainly because rain does not fall equally in all areas of a landscape—even within one storm. The amount of rain that is measured at one point can be quite different from a point even a short distance away—partly due to the actual amount that falls in different areas but also partly because of the design of the rain gauge.

There are probably two main reasons why you might want to use precipitation data—one related to rain and one to snow. In areas with small amounts of rainfall, it might be advantageous to collect rainwater for irrigation or domestic uses, and it's a fairly straightforward calculation to multiply the normal annual rainfall amount by the surface area that will be collecting it (say the roof of a house) to yield the volume of water that could typically be accumulated each year. In areas that receive snowfall, it can be valuable to know both the typical amount of snow in a given year and the direction of the wind during and immediately after snowfall events. This information would allow for strategic windbreaks to be designed into the landscape to encourage the snow to accumulate in desired areas and not where it is unwanted.

The distribution of precipitation around the world is fairly extreme. There are some areas of Chile that have not had precipitation in living memory. The lowest measured precipitation on earth is in Arica, Chile, where the average annual amount is less than one millimeter! On the other end of the scale, there are several places that contend for the wettest place on earth. The winner is probably Lloro, Colombia, where they get, on average, more than 13 meters (43 feet) of rainfall each year. Another way of measuring "wettest" is to count the number of rain days per year. This contest is likely won by a mountaintop climate station in Hawaii that has only about fourteen days per year when it *doesn't* rain. Lucky the person who selects those two weeks for their annual vacation!

Precipitation is a significant issue in many people's lives and livelihoods. It's certainly a rural tradition in Canada to record and compare rainfall amounts. Southern Saskatchewan doesn't get very much rain in a typical year—somewhere around thirty-six centimeters (fourteen inches), and most of that comes in the springtime.[4] Farmers at coffee row report on every rainfall event: "Wild Horse Butte only got a half inch." "We had a full inch on our north quarter." "Didn't rain at all at Shaunavon."

In terms of microclimate, though, it isn't so much the amount of rainfall but, rather, the time and duration of precipitation events that is often of most interest to us. Knowing that most of the rain in an area falls during a specific period allows for strategic planning. Elizabeth II, queen of Canada, once toured Saskatchewan to celebrate their one hundred years as a province. Anyone who looked at the average rainfall data for Saskatchewan would say that she could come at almost any time and expect clear weather—after all, they get less annual precipitation than places in the middle of the Sahara Desert. However, anyone who looked more closely at the rainfall distribution throughout a typical year would see that the month of May was smack dab in the middle of the rainiest time of the year. Sure enough, she came in May and spent her time under an umbrella, while the massive crowds stood in pouring rain, just about the only big rainfall of the year, to get a glimpse of Her Majesty.

With the other main form of precipitation, snowfall, we are more concerned about how much falls and what the direction and speed of the wind are during and after snowfall events. This will influence where and how much snow deposits in the landscape. The faster the wind is moving, the more snow it can carry with it. A light wind will hardly be able to deflect snow that is falling, and it will be distributed like a blanket across the landscape. However, a strong wind, either during snowfall or when there is snow on the ground, can carry it great distances and will deposit it unevenly across the landscape. When the wind slows down for some reason, such as behind a windbreak, the slower-moving air has to drop part of its load. Snow will build up in drifts behind windbreaks and snow fences. In winter landscapes, the deposition of snow can have a major impact on the lives and activities of the population. The champion of all snowfalls was during a week in February 1959 when almost 5 meters (about 15 feet) of snow fell at Mount Shasta Ski Bowl in California. Even the powder snow fanatics wouldn't dare ski in that much new snow!

We had a family business on Main Street in a small Saskatchewan town when I was a teenager, and one of my responsibilities was to clear the front sidewalk every morning before school. The sidewalk faced to the east and was often a relatively comfortable place to be, since the prevailing winds are from the west and the building provided a wind break of sorts. However, all winter long, the wind picked up snow from across the prairies and deposited it on my stretch of sidewalk. The reduced wind speed that made the area more thermally comfortable created ideal conditions for snow deposition. Across the street from me, the owner of the hardware store was itching to try out the various snow shovels and brooms in his store. Every morning I would see him come out, look at his snow-free sidewalk, sigh heavily, shake his head, and take his snow shovel back inside.

ENERGY BUDGETS

The energy budget is probably the most important concept in microclimatology. It is a powerful tool for analyzing components of the landscape to determine their effect on the microclimate. It's a fairly simple concept but can lead to some complex and insightful analyses.

Earlier, we discussed the concept of a radiation budget. You will recall that we said that all the radiation that reaches a surface has to be accounted for and that it can be intercepted, reflected, or absorbed. Now we are going to consider the radiation that has been absorbed by a surface. Once again, we have to say that all the energy has to be accounted for. So where does it go?

Radiant energy that is absorbed by a surface is divided first between two streams of energy. We can think of these two streams as lining up and taking turns. First in line is *latent* heat (that is, heat that is used to evaporate water). As long as an object is wet, and the atmosphere has some capacity to receive more vapor, evaporation can take almost all the energy that it wants from a surface—and changing the state of water from liquid to vapor takes a lot of energy! Wet surfaces will generally gobble up a lot of the energy they receive, and there will not be much left for the other stream. If the surface is dry, however, and if there is no liquid water available to evaporate, then no energy can go into evaporation and all of the energy has to be used by the other stream—*sensible* heat (that is, heat that can be sensed).

The molecules in the surface of the material become excited by the energy they receive, they become more energetic, and the temperature of the surface begins to rise. The molecules at the surface will become warmer than those molecules below them in the material as well as those above them in the air. If the object has a high capacity to absorb heat, then a large amount of energy will go first into the *conduction* channel—that is, it will be conducted into the material. Some materials, such as stone, have high thermal admittance values, so they will allow a lot of energy to be absorbed and used to warm the interior of the stone.[5] Other materials, such as wood, have low thermal admittances, so not much energy will be admitted into the interior of the wood.

The second channel through which the heated molecules at the surface can expend their energy is convection. As we have discussed before, air molecules that come in contact with the surface get heated and carried away by the wind or will rise because they are warmer than the surrounding air (a process known as *natural convection*). Finally, if any energy is left over, it will be emitted as terrestrial radiation.

Through this simple but powerful model, we can understand and control the energy of any surface. Let's consider a few examples. We've talked a few times already about how a black asphalt surface can get so hot on a sunny day. Let's use an energy budget to find out why.

First of all, the low albedo of the black color means that most of the solar radiation reaching the surface will not be reflected and will have to be absorbed. Unless there has been a recent rainfall, the surface will be dry and no energy will be able to go into evaporation. All the energy has to go into heating the asphalt itself. The surface will become quite hot, and this surplus of energy can be conducted into the asphalt, passed into the air by convection, or emitted as terrestrial radiation. A strong, cold wind would be able to cool the surface, but on a hot still summer day, a very large portion of the solar radiation received will heat the asphalt and be emitted as terrestrial radiation. A person standing on the asphalt surface would be bathed in a stream of terrestrial radiation.

If you wanted to manage the microclimate so as to reduce the terrestrial radiation emission, you have the opportunity to modify any or all of the channels. First, you could reduce the amount of solar radiation arriving at the surface by intercepting it along the way. This could be done with a shading device, such as a tree in full leaf or an overhead canopy. If you can't intercept the radiation, then you could change the albedo of the surface. This could be done by painting the asphalt a lighter color or in some way covering it with a layer of lighter-colored material. The next option you have would be to wet the surface to allow energy to go into evaporation. If you continued to add water to the surface, eventually it would cool down to air temperature or even lower. If the humidity in the air was low, the surface would cool down to the dew point of water. Finally, if none of these options is available to you, then you would need to consider whether you could use the terrestrial radiation. For example, could the asphalt surface be allowed to heat up during the day and then used as an input of terrestrial radiation in the evening when the air is cooler?

A few years ago, I was visiting some friends who live in the interior of British Columbia. The climate there can be very hot and dry during the summer, and their home had decks on the east and west sides of the house, both of which were completely open to the sun. We had coffee on the east deck early in the morning, but by midmorning it was impossibly hot. We were able to then move to the west deck until nearly noon, and then it too was unbearably hot. Then neither deck was usable until late in the evening, when the air started to cool. Both decks were quite comfortable then due to the amount of terrestrial radiation that they were emitting. The problem was that this pattern didn't match my friends' preferred use pattern. They really wanted to be outside in the afternoons and early evenings because that is when the house got so warm that it was uncomfortable. During the heat of the day, they had nowhere to go to be comfortable.

If you were faced with this problem and were asked to provide some design advice, you could consider the energy budget of the situation and provide a series of possible solutions. You might first suggest that the solar radiation be intercepted before it reaches the deck. This might be accomplished with a strategically placed shade structure or shade tree. Another option would be to intercept the solar radiation before it reaches the people on the deck. This could be done through the use of movable shading devices such as umbrellas, but the shadow of an umbrella would be offset by the angle of the sun—that is, when the sun was not directly overhead, the shadow of the umbrella would be cast some distance from the umbrella. Finally, the people themselves could be encouraged to wear light-colored clothing, which would reflect most of the solar radiation they receive, or they could hold an umbrella to shade themselves.

These techniques would be effective when the sun is actually shining on the deck, but the two decks actually offer an opportunity where one of the decks will be shaded by the house itself at all times except precisely at noon. This means that a shading device might not be necessary and that other means of cooling the decks could be employed. By mid-morning, when the sun is providing so much solar radiation on the east deck that a person would be too hot there, the west deck is shaded quite nicely by the house. The surfaces would have received little solar radiation since the previous afternoon so would likely be quite cool and emitting low amounts of terrestrial radiation. It is probably quite comfortable on the west deck until nearly noon.

Now the problem starts. After noon, the west deck has no shade and the solar radiation load is too large for anyone to spend any time there. Meanwhile, all the surfaces of the east deck are hot from the solar radiation load that they received all morning and are emitting huge amounts of invisible terrestrial radiation. Anyone sitting there would be uncomfortably warm. What opportunities are there for cooling the surfaces? The first thing to think about is whether a lot of the solar radiation that reaches the surface can be reflected. This could be done by lightening the surfaces' colors. White surfaces would stay quite cool, while darker surfaces would be much warmer. If there is no opportunity to lighten the colors, then what about changing the materials? Materials such as wood have low thermal admittance, so they will not store much energy and won't be able to provide a source of terrestrial radiation for long. Alternatively, brick walls, stone surfaces, and the metal of the barbeque will all have high thermal admittance values and will store a lot of energy that will be emitted as terrestrial radiation.

If you can't change the colors or the materials, what about a quick and effective fix by forcing the heat to go into the latent stream rather than into sensible heat? Water sprayed onto hot surfaces will evaporate, carrying heat away with it. If a surface is sprayed until it stays wet, then the surfaces will have cooled down to the dew point of the air, which is often lower than air temperature, especially in dry climates. The amount of terrestrial radiation it will be emitting will be greatly lessened.

Considering the energy budgets of surfaces in the landscape opens up a whole series of opportunities that might not have been apparent without it. There are many more areas that you will probably be able to think about in terms of the east deck, but let me suggest a couple more. First, we could introduce some forced convection into the deck by running a fan. If the fan were directed at surfaces, it would soon cool the surfaces to air temperature (remember our discussion about measuring air temperature, in which we purposely passed wind over a thermometer to make sure that it was at air temperature?). Used in combination with a spray of water, it would be a very effective way to cool surfaces. In addition, it could be directed at people, thus increasing their convective heat loss and making them feel cooler.

The final solution that I will offer for the east deck (although there are many more possibilities) is a weird one. So far I have been implying that all surfaces emit terrestrial radiation based solely on their temperature—that is, the warmer they are, the more radiation they emit. This is generally true, but there are a few interesting exceptions. Some materials are notoriously poor at emitting radiation, notably aluminum and gold. If you had two surfaces that were the same temperature but one was covered with aluminum and the other was something like wood or brick, the amount of terrestrial radiation from the aluminum surface would be much lower than the other surface. If you think about it for a minute, this begins to open up some interesting possibilities in the landscape. Aluminum deck furniture would reflect most of the solar radiation it receives and would emit little terrestrial radiation if it did heat up.

But, of course, the most effective action would have been to consider the microclimate when designing the house and decks in the first place—which is really the underlying intent of this book. Consider microclimate first, or at least very early in the design process, and you won't be faced with trying to resolve problems like this later.

Covering west-facing windows with aluminum foil has become a vernacular microclimatic design response. People do it to keep the interiors of their houses cooler in hot climates, but I'm sure that most of them don't understand the physics behind why it works. First of all it is highly reflective, so that most of the solar radiation that it receives it simply reflects away. That is quite effective in and of itself. However, there is the added benefit that when the air temperature gets very high, like it does in Tucson in the summer time, the temperature of the walls and windows of houses will also get very high. A normal glass window will emit radiation into a house based on its temperature, but an aluminum foil–covered window will emit terrestrial radiation at a much lower rate, resulting in a cooler interior to the house.

This concept was used in a spectacular way in downtown Toronto where a major bank constructed a tall office building. They covered the windows in gold. To look at the building from the outside, the windows are definitely gold colored, but in fact the layer of gold is almost unimaginably thin—just a few molecules thick. From inside the building, you can easily see out the windows as if there were no layer of gold on them. However, even a layer of gold that thin will emit at a much lower rate than the windows alone. This has benefit in both summer and winter. In summer, the amount of energy added to the interior of the building is reduced by the highly reflective gold. In the winter, the amount of energy emitted from the windows into space is minimized.

The concept of energy budgets can be usefully applied to other things in the landscape as well, such as buildings and people. As fossil fuel supplies dwindle and energy costs rise, the amount of energy needed to heat and cool homes will become of increasing interest to the public. An analysis of the streams of energy into and out of a building can help to identify ways to reduce energy loss in winter and energy input in summer. Similarly, assessing the flows of energy to and from a person in the landscape can help to identify ways that the environment can provide thermally comfortable settings. Sometimes, a problem offers an opportunity. The solar radiation that was making both the east and west decks too hot could be captured by solar panels, turned into electricity, and used to run an air conditioner to cool the interior of the house.

Remember the age-old question, "If a tree falls in the woods, and no one is there to hear it, does it make a sound?" We can ask a couple of similar questions about microclimate modification. "If a fan blows air through an outdoor area, and there is no one there to experience it, will it make the microclimate cooler?" or "If radiant energy is emitted into an outdoor area and no one is there to intercept and absorb it, will it make the microclimate warmer?" In both microclimate cases, the answer is no. It's like leaving a light on in a room when no one is there to use it. The light is only useful if there is an eye there to see it. Similarly, the tree falling in the woods sets up waves in the air. These waves are only experienced as *sound* by an ear, and if there is no ear to hear it, then there is no sound. Oh, and by the way, there is no color *per se* in the universe. It is the human eye that categorizes some of the wavelengths of the solar spectrum to allow our brains to experience them as colors. So it's all in how information is received.

SUMMARY

At this point, you might be asking the question that I've been asked so often: "so what?" What does it matter whether or not we can modify the air temperature or the humidity in the air and that the only things we can modify are wind, sun, and precipitation? Why do we need to understand that there is terrestrial radiation? If we can design landscapes that are thermally comfortable environments, why should we worry whether it is the air temperature that we are changing or the radiation that we are modifying?

The short answer is that if you don't understand what you are doing, you will be right only some of the time; the rest of the time, you will inadvertently create uncomfortable environments. If you find a pattern or prototype that works for a given climate region, you might be able to reproduce it over and over again and it might work reasonably well much of the time. But what if the site conditions are slightly different, or what if you move out of the climate region? What if your site was close to a large body of water? And what about changing a part of the pattern? Will you know for sure that it won't end up creating an uncomfortable microclimate? Unless you understand the physics of the system, you won't know how to correct it. Take the piazza situation in Italy: without considering the energy budget of the space, it is unlikely that anyone would have guessed that the cars parked there during the day were causing it to be a place where people didn't want to go in the evenings.

Or take a situation where people decide to make an outdoor café warmer in the cool evenings. If they didn't realize how quickly and effectively the air mixes and dissipates the heated air, they might end up wasting a lot of energy trying to heat the air. They might think that turning the heater on early would warm up the environment, when in fact it has no effect (except maybe to heat up the chairs and tables) until people are there to absorb it. Similarly, if they tried to warm up an area, they might not realize that as the air warms it rises out of a place and the energy is wasted. If they understood instead that a source of radiation will heat people in a cool environment without wasting any energy heating the air, they could create an effective and comfortable environment. There might be a situation where you would want to humidify the air—if you were doing a project in a dry climate, for example. Almost whatever you did would dissipate almost immediately. But if you understood the mechanism by which this happens, you could either decide to design to isolate the space from the surrounding air, thus creating an area of moisturized air, or you might try to achieve something else.

Here is an example that might help to make my case. As I began to formulate my ideas about the microclimatic aspects of the dry landscape gardens in Japan, I was interested in visiting as many of these gardens as possible to look for similarities. My Japanese colleague and I visited a garden that had been moved from its original location to a site outside Kyoto. The building and garden were meticulously moved, but when we sat on the verandah and looked into the garden, it was surprisingly devoid of any interest to us. It just seemed like a rectangle of gravel, and within a short time we were very uncomfortable and disinterested and rose to leave. It was at this point that we realized the orientation of the garden had been changed during the reconstruction. This garden had faced to the south when in its original location but now was oriented toward the north. The pattern was correct, but because the orientation was wrong, the microclimatic processes were very different, resulting in a garden that didn't work.

Here's another example. One landscape prototype that can be very effective is the *sun-catch*. This is a situation where the outdoor area is oriented on the south face of a hill or the south side of a building and wind barriers are provided on the west and north sides. A sun-catch can be thermally comfortable even in the middle of cold winter days. While people

Figure 3.10 This sitting area no longer exists. It was designed using a pattern that has been successful elsewhere, but because it was oriented in the wrong direction, it resulted in a microclimate that was terrible instead of wonderful.

outside the sun-catch struggle along in the cold wind, others can sit and bask in the sun-catch—away from the cold wind and in the intense winter sunshine.

If a sun-catch is going to be used in the summertime, then it needs to have a shading device, a role that can be played very nicely by a deciduous tree. If the tree is located within the sun-catch to the south of the sitting area, then it will not block much solar radiation in winter and will provide welcome shade in summer.

But what happens if you change a prototype a little bit? For example, a prototypical sun-catch was built on the University of Guelph campus and the designer apparently didn't understand the microclimatic mechanism. It was built with all the right characteristics and looked fine, but it was orientated in the wrong direction (see figure 3.10). You can see that all the elements are there; they are just in the wrong spots. The sitting area opens toward the north, so the sun doesn't shine into the area during the winter. However, the cold winds can blow directly into the space. In summer, the shadow of the tree falls on the walkway, while the breezes are effectively blocked by the windbreak. You would be hard-pressed to design a more microclimatically *inappropriate* space. Nobody ever used the space, and after a few years it was dismantled. If you visit it today, you will see that they have removed all the seating and covered it with turf. Now it is simply a maintenance problem.

At this point, let's pause to think about what we have learned in this chapter. Human thermal comfort is affected by air temperature, air humidity, solar radiation, terrestrial radiation, and wind. Air temperature and air humidity affect thermal comfort but can't be modified very much through the design of the landscape (with some notable exceptions). On the other hand, solar radiation, terrestrial radiation, and wind can all be greatly affected by the landscape, so they provide us with mechanisms that we can modify through design.

These three elements affect thermal comfort differently in different seasons. When designing places that will be used in winter, we should design first to reduce the speed of the wind and then do what we can to maximize solar and terrestrial radiation. For places that will be used primarily in summertime, we should design first to minimize the solar and terrestrial radiation and then do what we can to allow breezes to move through the area. One simple way to remember these relationships is through the acronym WW:SS, which stands for Winter Wind:Summer Sun. In the winter the priority is the wind, and in the summer the priority is the sun. In the spring and fall the wind and sun are of roughly equal importance.

Now that you are aware of the largely invisible components of the microclimate, you can use your body to experience and understand them at a deeper level. Whenever you move through any landscape, be conscious of your thermal comfort; as it changes, assess what mechanism is at work. Take time to stand near a sun-warmed wall on a cool day, or by a cool shady wall on a hot day. See how long it takes before you notice the effects of the terrestrial radiation balance. Visit public open spaces and watch where people choose to spend their time. In the spring do most people look for a place to sit in the full sun? Do they avoid windy areas? In the summer do they seek shade? Does an area that is hot during the day attract evening visitors?

I'm sure that you are already forming all sorts of ideas about how you can use this information in your designs to make outdoor places more thermally comfortable. Now that you understand the mechanisms, they will become second nature and in many cases you can design for thermal comfort by simply using your intuition. For more complex situations, you will benefit from having a process that you can follow. In the next chapter, we are going to learn about a process that you can use to strategically and deliberately modify microclimates to create thermally comfortable outdoor space.

4

MODIFICATION

One of my graduate students, Vivian, investigated how some people used their homes in relation to the climatic environment. When she asked them how and why they used the various rooms in their houses, she heard story after story about how various parts of their house were too cold to use in the winter or too hot in the summer, or that their yards were unusable for most of the year. Even when Vivian asked them to describe the reasons why they used or didn't use spaces, nobody mentioned anything about microclimate. Not one person. Not one comment. The final set of questions in her interview used the word *microclimate* and asked them specifically about things like sunshine and wind, and then they talked. And talked, and talked.

Microclimate hadn't come to mind for them, but once it was mentioned they had lots of opinions and ideas. They would love to add a sunroom on the kitchen. They would love to be able to rotate their house so that the sun came in the living room rather than heating up their bedroom and making it difficult to sleep on hot summer nights. They would also like to be able to turn their house so the snow wouldn't pile up on their driveway. The other side of the house, where no one goes, was snow free all winter. Some of the people had neighboring houses directly to the south of them that blocked the sun all winter, when they would like to have had access, but allowed the sun through in summer, when they would like to have had shade.

These issues not only affect the energy use in a house and the thermal comfort of the various rooms and outdoor areas of a home but can substantially affect quality of life. In one situation, a fellow had his business in his home. The only room that was available for his office was dull and dreary, cold all winter, hot all summer, and was generally a depressing place to work. It doesn't need to be that way. But, unfortunately for them and millions like them, these people have to live in homes that were not designed with microclimate in mind.

Knowledge and technology are available today to make homes and public spaces thermally comfortable, energy efficient, water efficient, and just generally wonderful living and working environments. Simply orienting a facility in the right direction can have a major impact. In the mid- to high latitudes, almost every building and outdoor space should be oriented toward the south. Much of the year in northerly sites, and some of the year in more southerly locales, it is cool enough to benefit from solar radiation input. And when you don't want or need it, it is fairly straightforward to intercept it or reflect it away. There are sufficient weather records for most locations now to help determine with some confidence where the winds typically blow from in the different seasons. Almost everything should be oriented away from the most prevalent winds in the cool and cold seasons, and toward the most prevalent winds in the hot seasons. This is normally quite possible, as winter winds often blow from the cold northerly and westerly directions, while summer winds are often southerly.

Beyond these basics, many, many other things can be done to make indoor and outdoor spaces more microclimatically appropriate. The colors of surfaces and objects can be modified to absorb more or less radiation. Materials with higher or lower thermal admittance can be used to strategically heat up or cool down surfaces in the landscape. Water can be added to cool surfaces through evaporation. Windbreaks can be strategically located to slow the speed of cold winds in winter. Conversely, faster-moving winds aloft can be directed to the surface through the use of sails or towers.

There are also ways to make people more comfortable in cool outdoor spaces, thereby extending the season of use. This can be done not only by making the spaces themselves warmer but also by making the person in the space warmer. For example, a radiation heater can be located so that the terrestrial radiation it emits can be intercepted and absorbed by people's bodies. Alternatively, outdoor spaces that are too warm can be made more comfortable not only by cooling the space but also by making people in the space cooler. A fan can be directed toward a person to increase convective heat loss. Surfaces can be sprayed with water to cool them, thus reducing the amount of terrestrial radiation being emitted onto people. And people themselves can be sprayed with fine mists.

What about the future of microclimatic design? It holds some intriguing and very realistic possibilities. In research, it is sometimes said that it is harder to come up with the right question than it is to come up with the answer. I've also heard it said that it is harder to envision what is needed than it is to invent something. Here are some ideas that might inspire you to invent a more thermally comfortable future.

Consider that in the winter, we would like to stop the wind and at the same time add heat to buildings and outdoor environments to make them more comfortable. What about designing something that will capture the energy of the wind, both reducing its convective ability and turning that energy into heat? Currently, wind generators take a lot of wind to make them turn, and the speed of the wind in the lee of a wind generator is not much different from that in front of it. In other words, current wind power generators do not remove very much of the energy from the wind. They are still fairly inefficient systems. How could they be made more efficient? Doing so would resolve two problems at once: reducing the cooling wind and adding desired warmth.

Summer offers a parallel situation. We generally would like to reduce the solar radiant input as well as to cool buildings and outdoor areas. In the future, maybe solar collection devices will capture enough energy from the sun and turn it into a source of energy that could be used to cool the air. This would remove the input of solar radiation and allow the energy to be converted into cool air. It could be as simple as a mechanical system that moves air down through a system of tubes in the ground to cool it during summer and heat it during winter.

There is enough energy going unused in every environment that there is no reason that homes and public spaces can't be completely energy self-sufficient and thermally comfortable. Mirrors could be strategically located and driven by computer-controlled motors so that the sun is reflected into or out of places based on energy needs, or onto devices that collect radiation (the way rain barrels collect precipitation). Much of the technology for this is available now and simply needs to be applied to public spaces or private homes. Consider, for example, the Italian village of Viganella, which is located at the bottom of a steep valley. During the winter, the surrounding mountains shade the main square. So they installed a huge mirror, eight meters by five meters (twenty-six feet by sixteen feet), on the hillside above the village. The mirror is computer controlled to move as the sun moves so that the sunlight is reflected into the square.

Structures that efficiently and effectively divert winds can be located and driven by computer-controlled motors to deflect wind into or out of places as needed. The interface between inside and outside could begin to dissolve. Like Japanese houses have done for centuries, houses could have removable partitions between rooms, and between inside and out. In the winter, the connection between inside and out could be mainly visual with good insulated windows, but there are also many ways to make outdoor spaces very livable even in cold winter climates. The key is not to try to warm the environment but, rather, to provide streams of energy that can be directed to a person in the environment.

I can imagine connecting a series of microclimate-modifying devices to a simple handheld control—sort of like a television remote control. One dial could work much like a thermostat in a house, except that, rather than simply increasing or decreasing the air temperature, the computer could determine the most effective means of cooling or heating people in an outdoor environment. If you are in the middle of a family barbeque and people are starting to feel too warm, turn down the dial. Depending on the weather conditions at that moment, the system might spray a fine mist onto the walls to cool them down and reduce terrestrial radiation loads. Need a bit more cooling? No problem. A fan might come on and provide some convective cooling on individuals. Need the big guns? The slats in the overhead trellis could rotate to completely block the solar radiation.

Design form would begin to rediscover regional identity based on climate, as each type has unique design strategies. The layout of streets in cities would reflect the regional climate. There are essentially four main climate types in the world when it comes to climatically appropriate design: hot and humid; hot and dry; temperate with cool to cold winters and warm to hot summers; and cold. The temperate and cold climates could be divided based on humidity, but the differences due to humidity are less substantial than they are in hot climates.

Midlatitude temperate and cold climates, such as in the northern United States and Canada and much of northern Europe and Asia, would benefit microclimatically from streets that run north–south and east–west and allow buildings to be oriented toward the south. Building lots would be laid out to encourage buildings that are longer in the east–west and shorter in the north–south direction to maximize solar access. Outdoor living areas would be on the south side of every house, and building heights would be regulated so that no one had to live in the shadow of a neighbor.

In equatorial regions, where orientation in relation to the sun is less of an issue because the sun is high in the sky in all seasons, street orientation has less effect on solar access. In these cases, street layout might respond to local topography or to local winds to allow air flow.

The widths of streets can also respond to the regional climate. In temperate and cold climates where solar access is desirable, the streets would be sufficiently wide, and the buildings sufficiently low, so that everyone has solar access in cool seasons. In hot and dry climates, the streets might be much narrower, and the buildings taller, so that the streets are in shade most of the time. The street layouts would be oriented according to the prevailing winds and connected so as to allow breezes to pass through relatively unobstructed. Where there is a local or regional wind, such as maybe a cool wind off a large lake or downslope winds off nearby hills or mountains, city streets would be oriented to allow breezes to carry the cool air deep into the city during hot seasons, while cold winds would be obstructed during winter.

As you know, slope and aspect of topography can have a huge impact on microclimate. Hilly topography provides opportunities for buildings to be set into the east, south, and west faces of hills—each of which would have a distinctive character and microclimatic environment. The east-facing slopes would be ideal locations for activities that have an early start to the day—schools, professional offices, day cares. The south-facing slopes would be ideal for homes to be built into the hillside so as to provide unparalleled insulation on the north sides while allowing solar access without obstruction from neighbors. West-facing slopes would be great locations for a variety of activities, such as restaurants with outdoor eating areas, and—in hot, dry climates—piazzas where people could gather in the evenings. North-facing slopes could be used for activities that have little relation to climate, such as factories and storage areas.

Design styles might emerge based on earlier vernacular or architectural styles. For example, a neo-prairie style of architecture might emerge in the middle of the North American continent, updating the already climate-sensitive style through the use of new knowledge, technology, and materials. Homes and urban areas in the far north could take on a distinctive style that would be informed by studying the traditional dwellings of the Inuit people. Homes in hot and dry climates would be informed by cave dwellings plus the cooling effect of evaporative cooling. Enlightened architects and landscape architects are already providing some of this, but much more could be done.

In addition to the practical advantages of microclimate modification, certain celebratory aspects should also be considered. Elements can be inserted into the landscape that interact with various components of the microclimate. Such elements include sundials, prisms, reflectors, wind deflectors, kinetic sculptures, wind chimed, windmills, and so forth. Every aspect of the microclimate can be brought to life.

I was walking through Bari, Italy, one day when I saw an elderly woman sitting on a kitchen chair, knitting. This wasn't unusual in and of itself. What caught my attention about the situation was that she was doing this in the middle of a very public piazza, nowhere near any residences. I found out that, day after day, she carries her chair from her home and sits in the same location. And it was a great location. The day was hot and sunny, like it often is in Bari, and her spot was very pleasant—cool and shady. Clearly, she had found a microclimate that she liked and had taken ephemeral possession of it.

In the evening, I would walk and talk with my Italian friends, along with hundreds of other people walking and talking. Italians tend to walk and talk—a lot. It's a wonderful social and cultural characteristic, and many designers have tried to replicate it through design of public spaces elsewhere in the world. On a typical hot evening in southern Italy, people come out to walk and talk and to gather under the shade of the few trees in their otherwise fairly gray and stark urban landscape (see figure 4.1).

One of my friends, Bill, came home from travels in Italy in love with courtyards. He lives in Thompson, Manitoba, which is located at about fifty-five degrees north latitude. During the winter in Thompson, the sun barely skids across the southern horizon for a few hours, and during the summer it stays up almost all night. I know this because I spent the better part of a year in Thompson as a young man working underground in the nickel mines. In the middle of winter, it was pitch black when I went underground in the morning, and it was pitch black when I emerged later that afternoon. I relied on local gossip to determine that in fact the sun had risen and set while I was underground.

This is not a geographic location that lends itself to building courtyard houses, but Bill persisted. His house looks quite Italian, but it doesn't function at all like the courtyard houses in Italy. Courtyard houses are intended to keep the occupants cool in a hot climate—and nobody would ever ac-

Figure 4.1   The hot, dry climate of southern Italy is ameliorated in the late afternoon by the shade of the palms. These men have gathered in the piazza to visit and perhaps play a game of chess.

cuse Thompson of being a hot climate. When the mercury dipped to −50°C (−58°F), Bill's courtyard house was absolutely ineffective in keeping him warm. The biting winds filled his courtyard with snow drifts. The white walls reflected away any solar radiation that did manage to reach the house. And Bill worried all winter long whether the flat roof was going to be able to hold up against the massive snow load.

You can probably think of similar examples of people building a style of house or landscape because of the visual aspects or because of nostalgia but that clearly is inappropriate for the local climate. The lesson is clear: don't import design ideas from other climate regions without understanding the need to adapt the design to the microclimate.

CRITICAL COMPONENT DESIGN

When I was a youngster, I watched with interest as some family friends designed and built an addition onto their summer cottage. They said that they had been thinking about it for a long time and knew exactly what they wanted so there was no sense getting an architect or a landscape architect involved. When it was finished, there were oooohs and aaaahs all round. But then a strange thing happened. After the initial flurry of activity, no one ever used the new space. It was cold and dark all winter, and hot and stuffy all summer.

A few years later, they decided that what was really needed was another addition. They knew exactly what they wanted (again), but this time I was asked if I could provide some input. I designed the new addition so that it would function microclimatically both indoors and out. I provided them with drawings illustrating what it should look like when it was done, and they happily passed them along to the person who was going to build it for them—their nephew. Now, the nephew was a builder who knew his materials and had lots of opportunities to find special deals—for example odd-sized windows left over from previous projects. He could build this addition for a lot less than anyone else could. He also informed the owners that designers are all alike—they specify things that don't match the materials that are available, and it makes things so much harder to build. He would build using standard-size materials and save them a lot of money and time.

Of course, they trusted him, and soon the new addition was complete. Some of the spaces functioned well from a microclimate point of view, but some of the "special deal" windows were odd sizes that either allowed sun in where and when it was not wanted or didn't allow sun in when it was wanted. He saved some material by making the overhang on the south side quite a bit shorter than the design, and both he and the owners agreed that this was a good savings. Why would they need a long overhang like that anyway? And so on. In the end, the south-facing deck with the overhead trellis was replaced with a much easier to build and more practical west-facing deck. The front door was changed to a very practical steel door (and he just happened to have one left over from a project that would cost them nothing) and was moved around to the east side of the building, as was the parking area. All this made it so much easier to build and would save some money as well.

I'm sure you can guess what effect these minor changes had. The west-facing deck is unusable (the owners now have put a small gas barbeque on a walkway around on the east side, which is very inconvenient but at least the space isn't blazing hot when they want to use it). The missing overhang over the south-facing windows doesn't block the sun in summer, so the interior gets too hot. The front door gets snowed shut in winter, and once that has been shoveled out they can start trying to liberate the car. They move the snow over into the area on the north side of the house, which is conveniently free of snow. I think you get the idea. While the addition looked *generally* like the drawing that I had provided, many of the microclimate modification functions that I had carefully worked out were lost.

Their lessons were not lost on me and led me to develop the idea of *critical component design (CCD)*. People will often want to make many of the decisions about their environments, and those decisions might not be ones that a designer is comfortable with—such as having a nephew do the construction using leftover materials. In the CCD approach, people are informed about which components of the design *must* be incorporated for optimal comfort and usability, which ones are in the best interest of the project and they *should* follow, and which ones really won't make a significant difference and are optional.

I used this approach recently when my folks asked me to design an addition for their home in Climax, Saskatchewan. My brother the carpenter was going to build it. I drew up some plans and marked very clearly on them the critical components. The length of the overhanging roof on the south side had been carefully calculated to maximize solar input during the winter and block the sun in the summer. The sizes and shapes of the windows were designed to ensure that solar radiation would find its way to the right places at the right times of the day and year. A few specific windows were identified as being able to open, so that cool breezes would be able to find a way in, and a way out, of the room. The color of the exterior walls was in the *should* category—I suggested that they be white to reflect more solar radiation onto the deck in the spring and fall but that another light color would be acceptable. The colors of the interior furniture and floor coverings were also *shoulds*. I suggested dark tones that would absorb solar radiation and warm up naturally in winter.

One of the *optional* elements in the design was the style. I suggested a Scandinavian style (my mother's family is Norwegian) with white walls, clean lines, and tending toward minimalism. They decided on a more contemporary style. My folks ended up with additional living space that functions well microclimatically, suits their tastes for colors and materials, and makes my brother look good for having built such a wonderful place.

CCD provides key characteristics that need to be included in order to create a landscape or a building that will have positive microclimates. Some designers might feel that this approach constrains their creativity, but my experience is that constraints often inspire the most creative designs.

PROCESS

There are many different ways that microclimate can be considered in design, but I would recommend that it be introduced into the design process as early as possible. I'm going to outline an approach to microclimatic design, but I am going to follow the concept of the CCD and provide you with only the key elements. I'll list the things that I think you *must* do and the things I think you *should* do. You'll find that, after a little practice, these steps will fit seamlessly into your own design process.

The steps go something like this:

- *Climate*. Accumulate and analyze published climate data to find out what the typical climatic conditions are that you can expect in different seasons and at different times of day.

- *Precedents.* Review regional precedents (successful built projects) so you can build on the knowledge and experience of others who have worked in your climatic region.
- *Site assessment.* Assess your site to identify characteristics that will modify the prevailing climate to create microclimates (for example, a south-facing slope will be warmer and drier than a north-facing slope).
- *Microclimate modification through design.* Determine the interaction between the site characteristics and the prevailing climate (through the use of models or diagrams) so you can see the climatically positive and negative characteristics of the site.
- *Communication.* Communicate your results to your client and decide together on a climatically appropriate design program.
- *Evaluation.* Monitor and evaluate the microclimates after construction.

Climate

You *must* start by accumulating and analyzing published climate information. Find a weather station near your site and acquire the *climate normals* for that station. This information is readily available online for many stations. The normals will show the climate patterns that have happened over a thirty-year period and can give you an idea of what kind of weather and climate to expect. There are many statistics included in the normals, but the ones that will be most valuable to you are air temperature (daily maximum and daily minimum for each month), prevailing winds (percentage of the time that the wind blows from each direction, both for the year as a whole and for each month of the year), and solar radiation (normally available as total hours of bright sunshine per year, days with measurable bright sunshine, and percentage of possible daylight hours that are bright sunshine).

Air temperature data are the most commonly reported measure and often listed in terms of averages: daily average, monthly average, average daily high temperature, and so forth. Consider for a moment that the average temperature on the moon is about −18°C (−0.4°F). That doesn't sound too bad—until you realize that the side facing the sun is at about 100°C (212°F) and the side facing away from the sun is at about −150°C (−238°F).

To provide a general idea of the climate through the year, there is some value in producing a table that lists the normal maximum and minimum daily air temperatures. Your table might look something like table 4.1.

I've selected two cities that are at approximately the same latitude, on the same continent, but one of which (Vancouver) is on the west coast while the other (Thunder Bay) is in the middle of the continent. Weather systems tend to move from west to east, so the air in Vancouver has typically just spent a long time passing over the very large Pacific Ocean, which tends to moderate its temperature. The air in Thunder Bay, in contrast, has spent a long time passing over a large, dry continent. As a result, Vancou-

TABLE 4.1   This table lists air temperature *normals* for two North American cities: Thunder Bay, which is in the middle of the continent, and Vancouver, which is on the west coast. The first number for each month is the average daily maximum temperature in Celsius, and the second number is the average daily minimum temperature.

	Thunder Bay T_{max}	Thunder Bay T_{min}	Vancouver T_{max}	Vancouver T_{min}
January	−8.6	−21.1	6.1	0.5
February	−5.6	−18.4	8.0	1.5
March	0.3	−11.2	10.1	3.1
April	9.0	−3.3	13.1	5.3
May	6.4	2.5	16.5	8.4
June	20.6	7.3	19.2	11.2
July	24.2	11.0	21.7	13.2
August	23.1	10.1	21.9	13.4
September	17.1	4.9	18.7	10.5
October	10.4	−0.5	13.5	6.6
November	1.7	−7.7	9.0	3.1
December	−6.1	−17.0	6.2	0.8

All temperatures are in degrees Celsius (°C)

ver's summers will be a bit cooler, and its winters quite a bit warmer, than those in Thunder Bay.

Winds are named for the direction from which they blow. A west wind comes from the west and flows toward the east. Climate stations often record the speed of the wind and the direction from which it is blowing. The wind is typically quite variable in both speed and direction, so the published values necessarily report averages. The data will often be summarized to indicate the percentage of time that the wind blew from each of eight or sixteen directions. Let's look first at the yearly data for Thunder Bay and Vancouver (see table 4.2).

You will notice that the highest values for Thunder Bay are in the westerly directions—southwest, west-southwest, and west—with easterlies as

TABLE 4.2 Yearly wind data for (a) Thunder Bay and (b) Vancouver indicating the approximate percentage of the time the wind blows from each direction.

	Thunder Bay	Vancouver
N	4	1
NNE	3	1
NE	5	4
ENE	7	8
E	10	22
ESE	3	11
SE	1	7
SSE	1	4
S	3	4
SSW	4	2
SW	20	3
WSW	9	4
W	13	8
WNW	7	7
NW	7	4
NNW	4	1
Calm	9	9

a secondary peak. In contrast, Vancouver's prevailing winds tend to be from the easterly directions—east-northeast, east, and east-southeast—with westerlies as a secondary peak. While this gives us a general sense of what is happening in these two cities, we know from our earlier discussion that the wind plays a much larger role in human thermal comfort in winter than in summer. It's the engine that drives convective cooling and consequently reduces the thermal comfort of people in outdoor areas when the air temperature is low. Knowing the prevailing wind directions in January, say, would be more valuable information. It would allow you to strategically locate windbreaks to slow the majority of these cold winter winds. So let's produce a table of the percentage of time that the wind blows from each of the sixteen directions in our two cities during January (see table 4.3).

TABLE 4.3 January wind data for (a) Thunder Bay and (b) Van - couver indicating the approximate percentage of the time the wind blows from each direction.

	Thunder Bay January	Vancouver January
N	3	1
NNE	2	1
NE	2	4
ENE	4	14
E	3	30
ESE	1	10
SE	1	6
SSE	1	4
S	1	4
SSW	2	2
SW	12	2
WSW	14	2
W	21	5
WNW	12	4
NW	9	2
NNW	3	1
Calm	9	8

There is a very clear pattern to the data. In Thunder Bay, almost 68 percent of the time the wind blows from the westerly directions (spread over the five adjacent directions SW + WSW + W + WNW + NW, centered on W). Now that's a prevailing wind! Windbreaks in Thunder Bay must be located on the western side of outdoor areas if they are to have an effect in midwinter. Add to that the percentage of time that the wind is calm, and your simple design intervention can create an environment where the winds are low and the outdoor place more thermally comfortable 77 percent of the time!

Vancouver's winds are almost as clear, but in a very different pattern. The prevailing winds are easterlies, centered on E, but with a smaller range than in Thunder Bay. In this case, only three wind directions (ENE + E + ESE) account for 54 percent of all the January winds, with E alone accounting for 30 percent of all January winds. If we include the NE and SE winds in our considerations (to allow a fair comparison with the Thunder Bay data), we now have 64 percent of the winds from these five directions; by including the calm winds, we can reasonably achieve low winds in outdoor areas 72 percent of the time in January in Vancouver with a single, strategically located windbreak.

To make these data more visual, both for your own understanding but also to show clients in support of your design, you can generate a diagram called a *wind rose*. You simply superimpose the data onto the face of a compass with each of the wind directions labeled. You can then quickly and easily see the prevailing westerly winds in Thunder Bay and the prevailing easterly winds in Vancouver (see figure 4.2).

There are many ways that this type of diagram can be used. If you are handy with data, you could easily generate a wind rose for specific situations. I mentioned earlier that I was involved in the site design for a hospital in Nova Scotia where they get very heavy snowfalls. You might recall that one of my concerns was to keep the area in front of the emergency department snow free even during heavy snowfalls. We generated a wind rose illustrating the percentage of time that the wind blows from each direction when there was at least 1 centimeter (0.4 inch) of snowfall per hour. This is

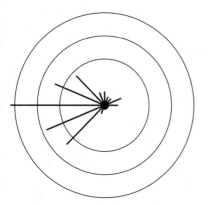 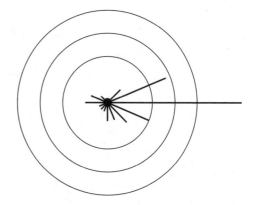

Figure 4.2 This wind rose illustrates the January wind data for Thunder Bay and Vancouver. This diagram was generated through a computer database program. You can easily see the prevailing westerlies in Thunder Bay and the prevailing easterlies in Vancouver.

sometimes known as *conditional climatology*, in that we set a condition—at least 1 centimeter of snowfall per hour—and selected only the winds that coincide with that condition. We also generated a wind rose for when there was at least 5 centimeters (2 inches) of snow per hour—in other words, during a heavy snowfall. These diagrams were central to making the decision about where snow would accumulate around the building (we'll talk more about how to do this a bit later) and which location would most likely be snow free so we could locate the emergency department there. Once you identify the potential problem or issue, you can often generate a wind rose diagram that will specifically address that situation.

Let's move on to discussing *solar radiation*. Climate stations measure and record information about the sun in a number of different formats, and it can sometimes be difficult to translate this data into a form that is usable in microclimatic design. Although some stations record and report solar radiation measurements, this requires a very sophisticated and expensive instrument. So most stations typically report solar radiation in one of three ways that will be useful in your design: the total hours of bright sunshine received each month, the number of days that experience at least some bright sunshine each month, and the percentage of possible daylight hours that receive bright sunshine (see table 4.4). The data can be illustrated in a number of different ways, of course, and I would recommend that you plot the data using a variety of graphing styles until you find one that makes it most understandable for you.

One way to understand the data is to relate it to a situation that you understand. For example, if you were originally from Vancouver and were doing a project in Thunder Bay, you could tell from table 4.4 whether it is sunnier or less sunny at different times of the year than you are used to. We can see that the total number of bright sunshine hours during the warm months of the year is quite similar in the two locations, but that during cold months Thunder Bay often has substantially more bright sunshine

TABLE 4.4 The solar radiation typically received at Thunder Bay and Vancouver are shown in this table in three ways: (a) the total hours of bright sunshine received each month; (b) the number of days with measurable bright sunshine each month; (c) and the percentage of possible daylight hours that received bright sunshine.

	Thunder Bay			Vancouver		
	a	*b*	*c*	*a*	*b*	*c*
January	114	23	42	60	18	22
February	134	23	47	85	19	30
March	159	25	43	134	25	37
April	219	27	54	182	27	49
May	265	28	56	231	29	49
June	264	28	55	229	28	47
July	283	30	58	294	29	60
August	258	29	58	268	29	60
September	163	26	43	199	28	53
October	128	26	38	125	24	37
November	89	20	32	64	18	23
December	92	21	35	56	16	22

hours than does Vancouver. It also has substantially more days during cold months with measurable bright sunshine. This is important information for design because solar radiation is an important input to the human energy budget on cold days. Much more solar radiation is available in Thunder Bay in winter than there is in Vancouver.

Precedents

Once you have an understanding of the prevailing climate, you *should* consider how people have adapted their designs to accommodate or modify that climate. One of the most valuable steps at this point is to identify the climate region using something called the *Köppen climate classification system*, developed in 1900 by Wladimir Köppen. World and regional maps illustrating these climate categories are printed in most introductory geography texts and can be found readily on the web. These maps are easily found on the web by searching for "Köppen climate map" or "Köppen classification map." This system will give you some key characteristics of the climate and will also identify other regions in the world that share that climate. For example, if you look up Toronto, you will find that it is a "Dfa" climate, which means it is a *humid continental climate with a hot summer.* This information can be valuable for getting a sense of an unfamiliar site as well as for considering precedents. For example, the climate in and around Toronto is in the same Köppen class as the Tohoku area of Japan, not far north of Tokyo. Precedent microclimatic design from this region of Japan has the potential for application in or near Toronto.

Boston also is within the Dfa climate class, so precedents there can be instructive when designing in Toronto. You might recall that the Boston City Hall Plaza is a large, open, windswept space that creates very unpleasant microclimates and is unused much of the time. Almost right across the street from it is the Quincy Market, which has wonderful, thermally comfortable outdoor areas. If you were designing an urban plaza in Toronto, you would definitely want to avoid the characteristics of the City Hall Plaza while embracing those of Quincy Market.

Site Assessment

Once you have a sense of the prevailing climate conditions of the area, and of the precedent design features of that climate region, you *must* familiarize yourself with the study site and its physical context. The most effective technique for doing this is to look at the site at different orders of magnitude. One simple way to do this is to follow the *rule of ten*. Take the largest horizontal dimension of your site, multiply it by ten, and consider your site in this context. Then take that number, multiply it by ten, and consider it at that scale. Continue this until your dimension is so large that you will be essentially considering the prevailing climate (the Köppen climate class). Let's illustrate this technique by considering the microclimate of a site where the property is one hectare with each side 100 meters, or 0.1 km, in length. Our design will consider the various microclimates on this site, but the first "context" to consider, following the rule of ten, is the landscape within a square that is 1,000 meters (1 kilometer) on each side. At this scale, you should be able to identify large buildings near your property or rows or trees that could impact on the *meso*climate that your site is in.[1]

Next, consider your site within a 10-kilometer context. This would identify large urban developments or large green spaces upwind or nearby that would result in a distinctive *miso*climate for your site. The 100-kilometer context would allow you to identify any large bodies of water in the region or any large topographic landforms that would create a unique *meso*climate. And finally, when you get to the 1,000-kilometer context, you will be basically looking at the *macro*climate, which is essentially what is being measured and recorded at weather stations and often coincides with the Köppen classification.

The context is very important to consider because, although we can modify some elements of the *micro*climate through design, most elements that affect the other scales of climate are not readily modified at the site scale. Some elements of the mosoclimate, for example, can be modified through neighborhood design, and some elements of the misoclimate can be affected by urban planning. For now we are going to assume that the four levels of climate are given and that we have to work within them to create thermally comfortable microclimates.

Let's look at a couple of examples of how context can affect the climate of a site and its potential use. Toronto is built on the shore of Lake Ontario, which rarely freezes over (so is warmer than the surrounding frozen land) and doesn't become too hot during the summer (so is cooler than the surrounding hot land). This results in a misoclimate near the water that is often quite different from the misoclimate in downtown Toronto or in the suburbs. In spring and summer, for example, the air temperatures near the water can be quite a bit lower than air temperatures elsewhere. Conversely, in winter, the air temperatures near the water are relatively higher than they are farther from the lake—for example, in the suburbs. This ameliorating effect of the water can have major implications in terms of outdoor activities.

As another example, Buffalo, New York, is just a short drive down the freeway from Toronto, and it is also located on the shore of one of the Great Lakes—Lake Erie. In winter, when the cold prevailing westerly winds blow over the unfrozen lake, they pick up massive amounts of moisture, which they dump on Buffalo in the form of snow. If you were designing a site in Buffalo, this misoclimatic or mesoclimatic condition would be a critical consideration. For example, large amounts of snow can be expected to accumulate downwind of a windbreak, so these areas would be appropriate for a toboggan hill or park but not for a major intersection or a shopping street. Areas where the prevailing winds are channeled between buildings would have much less snow accumulation and, although the wind would lower the thermal comfort of any pedestrians, they would be great places for parking lots.

Local winds can also be affected by large topographic differences, such as the mountains that almost encircle Tucson, Arizona. One of my graduate students, Jennifer, was gathering basic wind data for her design study in downtown Tucson when she noticed that there was a diurnal pattern to the local winds. The mountains that surround Tucson affect the wind through their thermal environment, causing winds to flow upslope during the day (known as *anabatic winds*) and downslope at night (*katabatic winds*).

These kinds of regional or mesoclimatic effects can have a substantial effect on the type of microclimate modification that can be achieved. And if you have ever visited Tucson in the summer, you can appreciate that a little cooling can go a long way. At the mesoclimate scale, the City of Tucson could decide to keep their washes (dry riverbeds) free from obstruction or development to allow the cool mountain air to flow down into the city at night. At the mosoclimate scale, this cool wind could be directed into neighborhoods and allowed to flow silently down the streets at night. And at the microclimate scale, individual homeowners could capture a bit of this cool stream of air as it passes and run it through their houses.

After considering the context of a site, you now must spend time on the site and experience the microclimates firsthand. This advice was given to me by the late Sir Geoffrey Jellicoe, who used to occasionally spend some time at our university giving lectures and talking with students. He was always generous with his time and advice and would host our students for an evening in his home on Hampstead Heath during our London semester. (As far as I know, he is the only landscape architect who has ever been knighted by Her Majesty, Queen Elizabeth II, for his professional work.) He told us that when he started a project, his preference was to spend time, a lot of time, alone on a site before he did anything else. He said that inevitably his clients would want to tour the site with him and point out everything about it and tell him what they wanted here and there. He said that he wouldn't be so rude as to tell them that he didn't want them along, but he said that he didn't really listen to what they said during the first visit. He said it was more important to just *experience* the site.

So after dutifully walking around with the client, he would go back to the site on his own. He would use all of his senses to experience the microclimates of the site. He described to us how he would smell the air, feel the breeze on his face, listen for the rustling of leaves, taste berries and seeds—and he would assess his personal thermal comfort everywhere he went. He would linger in places that seemed to have a positive microclimate, and he would try to determine what it was about the landscape that modified the wind, the sun, and the terrestrial radiation. Only after really immersing himself in the microclimate did he begin his formal assessment of the landscape.

When conducting an assessment of a site, the three elements that you must pay attention to are *topography*, *vegetation*, and *structures*. These three elements will have the greatest impact on the prevailing microclimate and will provide opportunities or present limitations on microclimate modification through design.

Knowledge of the topography of a site can be used to identify the angular relationship between the land and the sun, with the goal of illustrating the variation in intensity of solar radiation received across the land. In other words, you can show which places will be inherently sunny and those that will be shady.

When mapping topography, the two characteristics that need to be illustrated are *slope* and *aspect*. The more nearly perpendicular a slope is relative to the sun, the higher the intensity of radiation that will be received. The aspect of a slope, or the direction in which it is facing, can generally be mapped into four classes: east-facing, south-facing, west-facing, and north-facing. East-facing slopes will receive direct solar radiation in the mornings, south-facing slopes through the middle of the day, and west-facing slopes in the afternoon. North-facing slopes receive little direct solar radiation depending on the latitude of the site. Map the four classes with the north-facing slopes receiving the darkest tone, east- and west-facing medium tone, and south-facing the lightest tone.

For the other two key elements of a site, vegetation and structures, a good overview can often be generated by mapping areas into four main categories: *deciduous trees*, *coniferous trees*, *structures*, and *none of the above*. Deciduous trees will intercept solar radiation in summer but will drop their leaves in winter and by so doing will allow more solar radiation to pass through. Coniferous trees and structures will intercept solar radiation in all seasons. Areas with no trees will not intercept any solar radiation in any season. In terms of the wind, coniferous trees and structures will affect wind speeds in all seasons while deciduous trees will only reduce wind speeds in summer.

I wish I could tell you that there is now one supermap that can be generated that will answer all your issues around microclimate, but unfortunately there is not. There are many, many ways that the various maps can be analyzed. I would suggest that you first combine your slope and aspect map with your vegetation and structures map. Each area can be described based on the effect that it will have on the microclimate. For example, we know that south-facing slopes with deciduous vegetation have tremendous potential for use as housing or as outdoor use areas, such as parks and plazas. The orientation toward the south provides solar access, and the deciduous trees provide shade during the summer while allowing a lot of solar radiation to pass through during the winter. A steep north-facing slope covered in coniferous vegetation is going to receive very little solar radiation at any time, and the wind speeds will tend to be fairly low relative to the prevailing condition. This condition has severe limitations for use in microclimatically appropriate housing. There are ways to get around the inherent limitations, but at least you and the client should be aware of the limitations.

You should analyze your maps while considering the climate data that you recorded earlier. For example, if your site is in Thunder Bay, you know that the winds are primarily westerlies, so the areas to the east of coniferous vegetation will be shielded and the wind speeds will be lower there.

Now that you have a pretty good idea of the general microclimatic character of the site, it's time to meet with the client and find out what they are hoping to achieve. This is your opportunity to advise the client as to the best uses for the site in terms of the microclimate.

Microclimate Modification through Design

When you start to work on the design of a landscape, consider each of the elements in terms of energy budgets. Areas that are to be used by people should consider the energy budget of a person and identify the key times of year and times of day that they will be used. When you begin to plan the layout of the site, consider each program element in terms of what its ideal microclimatic conditions would be and see if there is an area that would best accommodate it. This requires that you think through how each facility would be used throughout the year.

Take the example of an outdoor café. It is important to know what times of day and what seasons it is intended to be used. The outdoor cafés in Tokyo near my home were intended primarily for use from late fall to early spring. They rarely get snow in Tokyo, and winters are mild enough that sitting outside is an option on many days. They also wanted to use them primarily in the afternoons and secondarily in the evenings. An ideal orientation for such a place would be on a west-facing slope, with wind protection from the north and west. The winter sun would warm the café and the patrons in the afternoon, and the warm surfaces would continue to emit radiation long into the evening. The terrestrial radiation load could be enhanced with strategically placed radiation heaters.

In contrast, outdoor cafés in Toronto seem to be places that people go mainly from spring to fall, with winters being considered to be too cold for such activities.[2] Here an ideal site would be one oriented toward the south, with wind protection to the north and west but quite open to the south and east. The early spring and late fall winds that come primarily from the west and north would be slowed, but the summer winds from more southerly directions would be allowed to pass through. Solar access would be appreciated in the spring and fall, while shade is a requirement in summer. This can be accommodated through the use of deciduous trees, vine-covered trellises, or movable shade structures such as umbrellas or canopies.

Evaluating the existing conditions on a site will identify prevailing opportunities and limitations. Once you begin to consider where facilities might be located on a site, you then have to start to think about how they are going to modify the existing microclimate. This is the time to identify *performance objectives*. Identify what you are trying to achieve, in terms of microclimate, with each facility. Everything that is done to a site will modify the microclimate in some way. There are various tools available to help you determine the effect that you are going to have on the microclimate. As discussed earlier, the two elements that you can affect the most are the solar radiation and the wind.

The effect that design will have on solar radiation can be identified through the use of shadow-casting tools. There are easy-to-use computer programs that will generate shadow diagrams, but it can also be done quite easily by hand. When you generate these diagrams, though, you have to keep in mind that the time that we see on the clock is almost certainly not the actual *sun time,* and you have to account for the difference. Before trains and remote communications, people tended to use just sun time in their daily lives—that is, when the sun was due south, it was noon, and all the clocks in one community would match this time. However, when the sun was due south in one community, a community to the west would still be experiencing morning—the sun would not yet have reached south. This wasn't much of a problem as long as people traveled by horseback or walked, and as long as communication was mostly by mail. However, this practice became problematic when people started to travel by train. Imagine the engineer setting his clock based on local time at the beginning of a trip, and then by the time he reached the first stop his clock would no longer match that of the locals. It became a real headache for scheduling travel.

Various schemes were tried to standardize time, and it was a Canadian, Sanford Fleming, who eventually proposed a system that seemed to work for everyone. He proposed twenty-four *time zones* that covered the entire earth. So, rather than the time changing slowly as you traveled easterly or westerly, it now jumped from one hour to the next at the edge of a time zone. If you drive from Toronto to Vancouver, every once in a while you have to turn your watch back by one hour. His suggestion was the basis for the system that is now used almost everywhere on earth.

This system works well for scheduling travel, but it has caused a disconnect between the movement of the sun and the time on the clock. The sun rises earlier at the eastern edge of a time zone than it does on the western edge. And for convenience, time zones are sometimes made broader or narrower based on political boundaries. For example, despite being a huge country, China has only one time zone. The equivalent distance east to west in Russia has four time zones. So if you are generating shadow diagrams for an area in western China, the time that is on the clock can be several hours different from sun time.

Things get even more complicated because of daylight savings time (DST). The middle of the day according to sun time is noon, but the middle of the day for many cultures is much later than that. So, rather than "wasting" daylight hours in the morning, when few people are up to appreciate them, the clock is adjusted by one hour in the spring, requiring people to rise an hour earlier—not a popular decision with night owls! But not everyone changes their clocks based on DST, and if you live near the edge of one of these zones it can be quite confusing.

It is probably a combination of politics and economics that has determined the time that the clock says in any given community, and you need to know the relationship between the clock and the sun. Otherwise, you might design an area for use during the lunch hour only to find that the sun shines beautifully into the space from 10:15 to 11:30 every morning and is completely shaded when people arrive for lunch. Despite the fact that it sounds difficult and confusing, it is actually fairly straightforward to figure it out. Here is one approach that will allow you to quickly and easily calculate sun time from clock time. Go to your local Internet weather site and note the time that the sun is rising and setting. Solar noon will be halfway between these two times. I just went to my local site and found that the sun rose at 6:30 this morning and will set at 8:10 this evening. This means that the sun will be up for a total of thirteen hours and forty minutes today. Halfway between sunrise and sunset, the sun will be in the southern sky, so half of the length of the day is six hours and fifty minutes. Add this to the clock time when the sun rose (6:30), and the result is that the sun will be due south at 1:20 p.m.—an important difference from 12:00!

The effect that design will have on the wind is much more difficult to identify. There are many diagrams, tables, graphs, and illustrations that show various characteristics of the wind in the landscape, but they can be difficult to interpret. When faced with a wide range of these diagrams and relationships, it can be very challenging to see how they relate to a landscape that you might be studying. Here is where I think we can use a process that has been the mainstay of murder mysteries for a very long time: the process of identifying the perpetrator. It might seem like a stretch, but let's give it a try. The first thing the detective usually does is to ask if the witness knew the suspect by name. The witness almost never does because then it wouldn't be much of a mystery. The next step is usually to have the witness look through photos of individuals who have a history of this type of crime and might be a suspect. This sometimes works, but often the detective has to use a final step that involves asking the witness to identify each part of the suspect's face in isolation. The witness looks through pictures of many, many different noses until finding one that looks most like the suspect's nose. Then the identification moves on to the eyes, the mouth, the hair, and so on. When all of these pieces have been selected, they are put together into a composite sketch of what the suspect looks like, sort of.

When considering the wind in a landscape, we can follow a similar process that I like to call the *composite wind analysis*. The first step, like asking if the suspect is known, is to ask whether the landscape you are considering is a typical situation for which we have equations to describe the wind. A flat landscape covered with mown grass is one such example. Most landscapes are too complex for these simple equations, so you will likely need to go to the second step. Similar to looking through photos of suspects, you can use the results of wind tunnel studies that either you commission yourself or that your client might have commissioned for another reason. For example, a colleague and I modeled the microclimate atop the proposed New York Times Tower in Manhattan. A wind tunnel study had already been completed to simulate the winds on the roof for other reasons, and we were able to reanalyze their results for use in our study.

But, like the murder mystery situation, in most cases you will need to consider how each component of the landscape will affect the wind and then piece the information together into a composite diagram that will characterize the wind on the site, sort of. Rather than using nose, eyes, hair, and so forth, you need to consider landforms, built structures, and woody vegetation. Each of these aspects will affect the wind, and when considered individually, some standard patterns that can be identified.

Start the composite wind analysis by looking at the landform. If it is relatively flat, then there is an equation that can be used to model how the wind changes with height, and there will be little horizontal variation in the wind caused by the topography. If there is a single, uniform hill on the site, it too can be characterized by an equation, but more readily by a simple diagram (see figure 4.3). If there is more than one hill on the site, this analysis can be applied to each one in turn, but the result will be only a rough estimate.

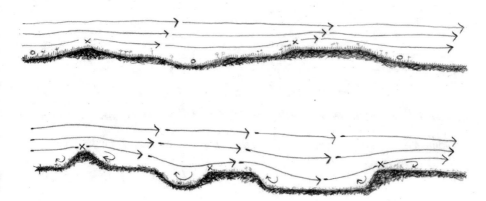

Figure 4.3 (a and b) These drawings illustrate the typical flow of wind over and around various kinds of hills in the landscape. The arrows indicate the direction that the air is moving. The "X" marks the location of the fastest winds, and the "O" the location of the slowest winds. Fairly straight lines indicate air that is moving primarily in one direction, while loops and convoluted lines indicate that the air is likely to be turbulent at this location.

The next step is to look at the built structures on the site. Consider the pattern and orientation of the buildings, and compare your result with the standard diagrams that illustrate wind flow around buildings (see figure 4.4).

The final step is to consider the effect of vegetation on the wind on a site. Look at the woody vegetation, and compare the patterns with the drawings in figure 4.5. The diagrams consider wind around individual trees, rows of trees, and walls.

After completing each of these analyses, you should draw them up like the composite sketch of the suspect in the murder mystery. Use arrows to illustrate wind flow on your site when the wind is from different directions, and identify areas that will likely have low, moderate, and high wind speeds.

In addition to designing for different uses, you should also consider the different users. For example, children in playgrounds can generate high levels of metabolic heat and require cooler microclimates than their parents, who are generating low levels of metabolic heat while sitting and

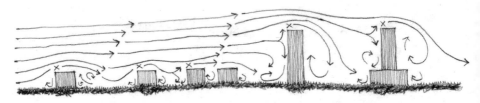

Figure 4.4   This drawing illustrates typical flow of wind over and around solid structures in the landscape.

Figure 4.5   This drawing illustrates typical flow of wind over and around trees and walls in the landscape.

watching. One of the expressions I have heard countless times in situations like that is that "a sweater is something that a child puts on when his or her mother feels cold." In fact, the child likely doesn't need the sweater, while the mother likely does.

.Another group of users whose requirements differ from the general population is the elderly. As people age, the rate at which their bodies respond to environments that are too hot or too cold slows considerably. The message that they are feeling too hot might not make it to the brain before they are actually so hot that they are experiencing hyperthermia. This situation, where their internal temperature becomes dangerously high, is much more common in the elderly than the opposite condition of hypothermia. People generally expect that they need to dress in warm clothing on cold days, but when it is nice and sunny outside they can easily put themselves in danger without realizing it. This has major implications for the design of facilities for the elderly—hospitals, assisted-living facilities, and so on. While it is important that the elderly have a facility that allows them to be outdoors, it is critical that the microclimates of those outdoor areas don't put them in danger.

Communication

During a two-week wilderness canoe trip in the Rocky Mountains, we inadvertently left one of our main food sources, a slab of maple-cured bacon, inside a plastic bag and inside a warm backpack for a couple of days. By the time we discovered our mistake, the bacon was quite ripe and was just on the edge of going bad. We knew that without it we might have some hungry days ahead, so we decided to leave it in the sun to dry and hopefully become edible. We put the bacon on top of our packs in the middle of the canoe and paddled blissfully down the mountain stream. After a few hours, it seemed as if the bacon was drying out and would be recoverable, so we were feeling pretty good about things.

Then we experienced one of those rare moments when we saw a very elusive animal in its native habitat: a grizzly bear. At first, we were delighted as we watched the grizzly trundle across the alpine meadow, stopping every once in a while to throw his snout in the air and turn his head about, snuffing deeply. He was following the scent of something, and slowly we began to realize that this massive carnivore was smelling us! Or, more specifically, smelling our bacon! This was no longer a wonderful wilderness experience; it was now an issue of survival. The grizzly's motivation was to find meat to eat, and we were clearly on his menu.

These massive beasts spend a large part of every year in hibernation, and when they emerge in the spring they are hungry, very hungry. And grumpy. They have a short few months to eat enough food for the whole year, and it is well advised to stay out of their way. They have a voracious appetite that apparently becomes insatiable when the salmon swim upriver from the Pacific Ocean to spawn in the mountain streams. It is essential to their survival that the grizzlies eat as many salmon as possible, so even when there bellies are full they keep eating. The more fat they can store in the fall, the better their chances of surviving a winter in hibernation.

This story is probably not unfamiliar to you, but think of the implications if, over a few million years, grizzly bears developed larger and larger brains and at some point far in the future became conscious. Now, imagine those grizzlies building cities, living in houses, having jobs, trimming their toenails, and buying their groceries in a supermarket. Every winter, without knowing why, they would feel this very strong urge to go to bed and sleep all winter. Getting up on a winter morning and going off to work would be a real drag! And every summer, they would get this insatiable urge to eat and eat and eat—preferably salmon—and they would gain prodigious amounts of weight. No matter how hard they tried to diet throughout the rest of the year, they would always gain it all back every fall.

Now cast your mind back to a time almost five million years ago, and imagine a hairy primate trundling through the arid savannahs of Africa, hunting meat and gathering fruits and vegetables. Over the next four and a half million years or so, these primates adapted exquisitely to their environment. Any individuals who didn't adapt died and did not pass along their genes, and slowly a new species developed, emerging apparently about

250,000 years ago as a big-brained, conscious human. While we didn't gorge on salmon every fall, we did evolve characteristics that allowed us to survive in the arid savannah landscapes in Africa at the time.

The biological evolution of humans is written clearly in the fossils and in our genetic code, and we can use this understanding to design environments that meet the habitat needs of humans. The thermal comfort need of humans is a consequence of the species developing in a very warm climate. Thick hair over our whole body was not an asset, and hairless individuals had an advantage. When those hairless primates moved to climates that are not warm year-round, they had to find ways to survive. And as people evolved physically, they also evolved means of communication. It is worth our while to find ways to communicate today that tap into the long-evolved preferences. When we are communicating ideas about microclimate and thermal comfort to clients, we can use lessons from evolution to ensure that our message is clearly communicated in a manner that is readily understood and appreciated.

Many other characteristics are widespread in the human population that probably are a result of natural selection. It is human nature to have a fear of spiders and snakes—something that would have been an obvious evolutionary advantage. While storing fat for lean times and being afraid of spiders and snakes have limited relevance in landscape architectural design, some other human evolutionary characteristics most certainly are relevant. Understanding the evolutionary motivations of humans can assist in many ways.

Let's now look at some of the characteristics of human nature that are relevant to landscape architecture. Remember where humans lived while they evolved—in the savannah landscape of Africa. Virtually every study that has investigated visual preference in the landscape has found a strong preference for savannah-type landscapes—that is, trees intermittently poking out of a grassy plain. It sounds like just about every suburban neighborhood in North America, doesn't it? So, this is probably not a passing fad, and it probably can't be changed very easily—it's humans' natural habitat, and it's human nature to prefer this type of environment.

In addition to having clear visual preferences, humans are also able to learn some things more easily than others. Even though car accidents kill far more people every year than spiders or snakes, it is far easier for humans to learn to feel safe in a speeding car than to feel safe holding a spider or snake. Knowing about these propensities allow us to work *with* human nature rather than trying to force people to do something that is against their very nature.

People living in urban environments seem to have a desire for contact with nature and for spacious, green, quiet landscapes. They also typically want to communicate with others about people and their actions—in other words, they like to gossip. Some studies have suggested that almost three-quarters of all conversation is gossip, and the preference is for face-to-face gossip. There is a strong propensity in humans to gravitate toward common ground and semipublic spaces. The apparent need for so-called personal space is a consequence of living in an urban environment that doesn't feel like natural human habitat.

A strong desire for *trade* also pervades human life. Even small children display trading characteristics in much of their play. Humans seem to need to trade, and places for this to happen should be accommodated in the urban landscape. This is also a characteristic that could be used to your advantage in negotiations with a client. They might be willing to consider trade-offs, giving up something to get something else, more readily than they would be willing to simply give up something.

There is a strong urge to be part of a group of about a dozen individuals—whether an extended family, a sports team, or a work group. Various studies over the years have found that there also seems to be a preference for being part of a community of about 150 individuals—the typical clan or tribe size of our evolutionary past. These become powerful guidelines to use in designing urban environments.

When interacting with clients, you should keep certain characteristics in mind. People tend to make decisions very quickly, and these are often based not on rational judgment but, rather, on first impressions.

When meeting with a client for the first time, dress smartly, carry yourself well, carefully determine what comments you will make early on in the conversation, and have some stunning visual images to share with them from the start. You will tend to find that people get a lot of satisfaction from working together with individuals that they see as being similar to themselves, so don't set yourself up in an adversarial position; rather, find areas of common interest. People will tend to make so-called in-group versus out-group distinctions, so they will be more interested in working together with you if there is a common *enemy* (such as the city bylaws). In general, people tend to be optimistic even when things are not going all that well, but they have a strong aversion to negative feedback. Positive comments and feelings can be undermined very quickly by one negative criticism.

When suggesting design options, offer elements that fit into humans' natural habitat and will be readily acceptable based on human nature. Include contact with nature; spacious, green, quiet environments; and elements reminiscent of savannah landscapes. Show images to the client that evoke these deeply ingrained feelings. Offer common grounds and/or semipublic spaces where groups of up to a dozen or so can meet and gossip. Provide spaces for trade and commerce. Explain that the spaces that you are offering will be thermally comfortable and will attract others the way an oasis in the desert attracts travelers. In the same way that good landscape architectural design works *with* the natural environment rather than against it, it also works *with* human nature and not against it.

Discuss the design not only with the person who owns and is building the project but also with people who will be using the project after it is completed. Sometimes this will be one and the same person, but often this will not be the case. Public projects should have public involvement, and development projects should consider the end user. When meeting with the public, divide the jurisdiction into communities of no more than 150 individuals and meet with each of these communities. During the meetings, further divide participants into groups of about a dozen, and try to form groups of individuals who have something in common so they will think of one another as friends. When the various groups report back to the community, find common ground and possibly a common enemy to draw the whole community together. And *listen* to what they say.

Evaluation

When physicians prescribe pills for an illness, they have you check back later to confirm that it was effective. There are also many researchers constantly testing the effectiveness of different drugs and treatments. When engineers build bridges, those bridges are monitored over time to ensure that they will continue to hold up to the traffic using them. But it is very common for landscape architects to complete a design and then never evaluate its effectiveness in any way. Some things about a design are very difficult to test, such as how much the public likes a new plaza or how many people typically use a park in the summer. But microclimate measurements are relatively easy and inexpensive to take and you should do it. I would encourage you to set up a simple monitoring station after construction and record measurements that will allow you to evaluate the effectiveness of your design.

Purchase a good-quality instrument package that measures air temperature, humidity, wind speed and direction, and some measure of solar radiation. Make sure that the package includes a recording device because the main measure of the effectiveness of your design will come from comparing your measurements—the microclimate conditions, with those same variables recorded at a nearby weather station—the macroclimate conditions.

Identify the key microclimate objective of your design, and use the instrument package to test how effectively you were able to achieve this. For example, if you were attempting to extend the season of use of an outdoor café into the spring and the fall, then set up the instrument package in late summer and let it collect data for a few days that include at least one sunny and windy day, and at least one cloudy and cool day. Then set it up again in the very early spring, and let it run through a cycle of weather that includes cool, sunny spring days as well as some cloudy, damp spring days.

Once you have the data, compare it with the data recorded at a nearby weather station. There are two very important things to remember when you make this comparison. Don't forget to do these, or the comparison will be meaningless. First, make sure that the time recorded on your instruments is the same as that recorded at the weather station. Duh! While it seems obvious, it might not be the case. Some weather station data uses "solar time," which can be quite different from "clock time." Remember that with time zones and daylight savings time, the time that we see on the clock can be quite a bit different from sun time.

The second important thing to remember is related to the height of the wind instruments above the ground. Weather stations typically record wind at 10 meters (33 feet) above the ground, and the wind here is normally quite a bit stronger than it is down at 1.5 meters (5 feet) above the ground, where you should set up your instruments. Make sure that you adjust the weather station data so that it is a fair comparison with your on-site data. This can be done quite simply by taking the table of wind speed values and running it through the following equation:

Wind speed at 1.5 meters = 0.7 × wind speed at 10 meters

In other words, the wind at 1.5 meters above the ground at a weather station is approximately 70 percent as strong as it is at the 10-meter measurement height. The resulting values will allow you to do a fair assessment of how your microclimatic design has affected the wind.

Generate graphs that illustrate the values of air temperature, humidity, wind speed, wind direction, and solar radiation over time. Depending on a number of variables, including how far your site is from the weather station, you might not see much difference in air temperature or humidity, but you should see the desired differences in wind and solar radiation.

EXAMPLE

The *New York Times* has been a major component of midtown Manhattan for a long time. You probably know that spectacular New Year's Eve celebrations have been held in Times Square for more than a century, and you might know that recently the *New York Times* decided to build a new headquarters. They hired one of the most famous architects in the world, Renzo Piano, to work with Fox and Fowle Architects of New York on the design of the building. One of the exciting and innovative ideas that they proposed was to grow a forest of birch trees on top of the building—a building that was scheduled to be one of the tallest buildings in New York. The vision was that the millions of people flying into and out of New York would look down on the city and say "there's the Empire State Building!" and "I see the Statue of Liberty" and "There's the New York Times Building with its birch forest on the top!"

The building was also going to have a ground-level courtyard, enclosed on all sides by the building but open to the elements at the top, and it too was going to have birch trees. Birch trees, as you likely know, are spectacularly beautiful trees. The bark is very white and peels off in paper-thin layers that curl and flap in the wind, and their leaves are a delicate green color in spring and a stunningly beautiful yellow in fall. In the winter, their stark white profile looks terrific against the dark background of a cedar hedge or a dark wall. It was a great idea for a wonderful building.

A landscape architecture partnership between Henry White of New York and Cornelia Hahn Oberlander of Vancouver was assembled to *make it happen!* One of the first things the design collaborators said to themselves was—wait a minute!—is the microclimate going to allow us to grow birch trees? They will grow only in full sun. Would the garden court in the middle of Manhattan provide enough solar radiation? Would the rooftop have sufficient access to sunlight for birch trees? At this point, my colleague Rob LeBlanc and I were invited to join the team. Microclimatic assessment and design were clearly going to have an important role in making sure that the signature birch forests of the new building were going to survive.

We followed the steps in the microclimatic design process I just described. I won't bore you with all the details but, rather, will provide an example of each stage of the process.

We collected prevailing *climate* data from New York. We were fortunate to be able to access data that had been collected at Central Park along with data from the airports in and near New York. We graphed air temperature, humidity, wind speeds and directions, and solar radiation and then adjusted it for our site.

In terms of *precedents*, we reviewed the literature on rooftop gardens, particularly those that included large trees. From this we put together an extensive list of potential rooftop trees and their environmental requirements, focusing of course on the paper birch tree (botanical name, *Betula papyrifera*). We determined that the paper birch was within its natural range in New York, and we noted the key characteristics required for its survival—most importantly, that it requires lots and lots of solar radiation. Paper birch will die if it doesn't get enough solar radiation.

Our *site assessment* was a bit unusual as we couldn't actually visit the site, which at the time was a lonely patch of empty air high above Manhattan. We did, however, note the height of the building, and we considered the context at the various scales. At the mosoclimate scale (within 1 kilometer [0.6 mile] of the site), virtually the whole area was dominated by tall buildings and urban infrastructure. We developed a three-dimensional computer model. This allowed us to move the sun through the virtual sky to see where the sun and shade were and to calculate how many hours and what intensity of sunshine the various locations could be expected to have. We used a very sophisticated modeling program because we needed to know the intensity of the solar radiation in various locations, but you can do almost as well by using the free, easy-to-use program called Google SketchUp (I hope it's still free when you read this). You can even easily import a Google Earth satellite image into SketchUp and build your model right on the image. This can be a very powerful and effective way to communicate shadow casting to a client.

The *microclimate modification* inherent in the site was primarily due to the height above the ground and to the effect of the adjacent buildings. You might recall that air temperature drops off at about 1°C per 100-meter rise in elevation. The rooftop of the New York Times Tower was going to be almost 250 meters above the ground, so temperature values were reduced by 2.5°C. We put together a composite wind analysis, but we also used wind tunnel data. Then we ran a solar simulation on the three-dimensional model of the area near the proposed building and generated maps that illustrated the number of hours of full sunshine that every part of the site received at different times of the year.

Communication became a bigger challenge than we had expected as the project was just getting rolling when the terrorist attack occurred in Manhattan. We ended up communicating much of the information through computer simulations, illustrations, phone conversations, and e-mails. Based on feedback from other members of the design team, it was apparently the graphic simulations that communicated most effectively. When the clients and the other designers saw the simulation of the sun moving through the sky, and saw how dark and shady many of the spaces were, it was clear to everyone that the green spaces in and on the building were not going to be easy places to grow birch trees.

The *design* stage was exciting and fun. After viewing the simulations and seeing our analysis, Renzo apparently said something like, "I can see that these are not ideal places to grow birch trees, but I still want birch trees in my design." What a terrific challenge! Based on the microclimate analysis, we generated tons of ideas about how to provide the birch trees with more solar radiation and better habitat. We proposed a large mirror on a servo motor that would follow the movements of the sun and reflect solar radiation into the shady places. We proposed using trees that look like birch but are not. But one idea emerged that carried the day. When we viewed the solar simulations, we had the idea of generating a map of the solar radiation that would be received at the canopy level of young transplanted trees rather than on the ground. Then we raised the simulated level of the canopy to the height of a full-grown birch tree and suddenly realized that mature birch trees would receive enough solar radiation to survive, if we could just figure out a way to get them to grow to that size. Then we hit on it: let's install mature birch trees!

Well, you can imagine that it caused quite a stir in Manhattan when a flatbed truck loaded with mature birch trees with massive root balls was driven into midtown. Then a huge crane arrived and the trees took flight, being lifted high up and into the courtyard.

The microclimate analysis provided us with another terrific opportunity: the area under the birch trees was an ideal location for a rolling green carpet of sedges and ferns. Visit the courtyard of the New York Times Tower and you will see this spectacular combination. By installing mature birch trees, we were able to provide them with the solar environment that they need, and at the same time the ground level, being so shady, provided ideal habitat for sedges and ferns. You can visit and see it for yourself. A birch-sedge-fern garden, right in midtown Manhattan!

The rooftop gardens provided an even more interesting and challenging environment. We had to find ways to reduce the high winds (remember that winds increase with height above the ground, and the rooftop is at 250 meters [820 feet] above Manhattan) while maintaining solar access. This led to my favorite part of the project: designing the rooftop gardens so that they would provide thermally comfortable outdoor environments for as much of the year as possible. We used COMFA, the human thermal comfort model that Terry Gillespie and I developed. We used the climate data to identify *typical days* for each season, which we used to test the kinds of conditions that could be expected at different times through the year. The model was used to estimate the thermal comfort levels of the prevailing conditions on the roof. Then various landscape elements were added and tested—trees, overhead screens, site furniture, and so on—and the computer model was used to estimate thermal comfort conditions as they would be modified by these elements. The results were compared with the prevailing conditions to see if the design interventions made the spaces more or less comfortable for people. As a result, the final design is a finely tuned microclimate that should provide thermally comfortable outdoors conditions on most days of the year—even winter!

I'm planning to wait a year or two after construction and then set up some instruments to see how accurately and precisely the models were able to predict the effects of the landscape on the microclimate. I'll also plan to spend some time there in different seasons and watch how people use the different spaces.

SUMMARY

Now that you know how the design of the landscape can affect the microclimate, and how the microclimate can affect the thermal comfort of people, you have the tools necessary to evaluate the effectiveness of built landscapes in creating thermally comfortable outdoor spaces. The next time you see an outdoor area full of people who are clearly enjoying themselves, take a few moments to consider their thermal comfort and what might be affecting it. You might want to join them and use your own body to assess how thermally comfortable you are in the space. Then look carefully at the landscape to see how it has been designed to create those conditions. Is there a windbreak, and if so which direction of wind does it affect? Have trees been strategically placed to provide shade on hot days? Have any sitting areas been located in thermally comfortable locations? And if you come upon an outdoor area that seems as if it should have people in it but does not, assess the microclimate of the space to see if that might be the reason. If it feels uncomfortably cool or warm, look around and see if you can determine what is causing it. Is the space completely shaded by a tall building? Does the wind get channeled between two buildings? Is it too open to the sun on a hot day? The lessons learned from these exercises can be invaluable when designing other outdoor spaces.

If a project is fairly simple and straightforward, you can often use the intuitive approach that was described in the previous chapter. For projects that are more complex, that are in a climate region unfamiliar to you, or that have thermal comfort as a stated goal, you should consider using the more complete and deliberate process described in this chapter. And the next chapter is going to give you one more approach. It summarizes and consolidates the information in this book into principles, guidelines, examples, diagrams, and tables, all of which you can refer to while designing thermally comfortable outdoor space.

5

Principles and Guidelines

Microclimate is not a particularly popular topic among designers, and it's not clear why. Evolutionary psychology seems to be providing some insight into this. There are principles that can be used to communicate your ideas in a way that enables people to understand and appreciate their value. It might be a combination of the topic's complexity, a lack of demand from clients and the public, and the fact that most things about microclimates are essentially invisible—or it might simply be that there is no clear and obvious connection between microclimate and human motivations that have evolved over millions of years. Despite these limitations, I would encourage you to always consider microclimate early in any project, and to make a convincing argument to your client as to why microclimatically appropriate design will be to their advantage.

There are times when I will read books cover to cover so I can thoroughly understand the theoretical foundation as well as the applicability of the information. While I might understand everything in the book at the time, I don't always remember all the details, and when I need to recall some specifics about that information at some later date I sometimes find it frustrating to sift back through the whole book looking for a few key points of information. I wish there was a chapter where the key information was summarized and easily accessed. That's what this chapter is for. Most of the key principles and guidelines that have been discussed in some detail throughout the book are summarized here. In addition, much of the information from the book has been applied to practical examples. Want to know how different landscape elements affect microclimate? Need to recall which elements of microclimate can be modified by the landscape? Wonder what a prototypical house and yard might look like in a temperate to cold climate? It's all here, and without all the extra words getting in the way.

MAIN CONCEPTS

1. The sun provides the main source of *heating* for objects in a landscape. The sun moves in a very predictable way through the sky. The amount of warming in various parts of a landscape can be changed through selection and placement of landscape elements, but it is much easier to reduce the input of warmth than to increase it.

2. The wind provides the main source of *cooling* for warm objects (such as people and houses) in a landscape. It moves in a somewhat predictable way through a landscape, and the amount of cooling in various parts of a landscape can be changed through selection and placement of landscape elements, but it is easier to lessen the cooling than it is to increase it.

3. Air temperature and humidity cannot be modified very much by the landscape, except in specific circumstances.

4. In summer, you can generally have the biggest impact on the microclimate by reducing the solar radiation absorbed by an object. In winter, you can typically have the biggest impact by reducing the speed of the wind that blows on a warm object. In spring and fall, solar radiation and wind are fairly similar in their effect, so you will have the biggest impact by reducing the wind while not reducing the solar radiation received.

5. When thermal comfort of people in the landscape is of primary interest, think of (a) the heat added to a person (mostly due to solar radiation and terrestrial radiation received) and (b) the heat car-

ried away from a person (mostly due to wind and terrestrial radiation emitted).

UNDERSTANDING AND MODIFYING RADIATION

1. The sun provides solar radiation that adds "warmth" to elements in a landscape.

2. The sun rises in the eastern sky, travels to its highest point in the southern sky, then sets in the western sky, describing an arc. Its position can be readily determined for any time of the day and the year using charts or computer programs, and this information can be used to determine the length and position of shadows that landscape elements will cast.

3. The arc of the sun is highest in the sky in summer and lowest in winter. In summer it rises in the northeast and sets in the northwest, while in winter it rises in the southeast and sets in the southwest. The sun is always due south midway through its arc, and the southern sun is highest in the sky in summer and lowest in the sky in winter. The difference in elevation of the noontime sun between winter and summer can be quite large.

4. The more perpendicular the sun's rays are to the surface of an object, the higher the intensity of radiation received by the object.

5. The darker the color of a surface, the more solar radiation it will absorb and, in general, the hotter it will get and the less it will reflect solar radiation onto other surfaces. Conversely, the lighter the color of a surface, the less it will absorb, the cooler it will stay, and the more it will reflect solar radiation onto other objects.

6. Everything in the landscape emits terrestrial radiation. In general, the higher the temperature of the object, the more radiation it gives off (with a few notable exceptions).

7. The sun moves faster through the sky in summer than it does in winter.

8. Clear sky emits very little terrestrial radiation compared with other surfaces in the landscape.

UNDERSTANDING AND MODIFYING WIND

1. Wind is generally the most effective tool for "cooling" objects in a landscape. It will remove heat from objects *until they are the same temperature as the wind*. The wind cannot make things cooler than it is itself. However, if an object is wet, evaporative cooling can lower its temperature to below air temperature.

2. Wind is quite variable in the landscape as it can blow from any direction. However, there are often patterns that can be identified and used. Winds in any given region will tend to blow from some directions more than from others (often called the *prevailing winds*). The prevailing wind often changes with the seasons.

3. Winds can be slowed through strategic placement of elements in the landscape. Vegetation with about 50 percent porosity generally is the most effective windbreak in the landscape. Windbreaks that are less porous than this will generate turbulent air, which adds to the cooling effect of the wind.

UNDERSTANDING AND MODIFYING AIR TEMPERATURE AND HUMIDITY

1. The temperature and humidity of the air are not affected very much by the landscape at the microclimatic scale. However, on cold, clear nights, air exposed to the open sky can become much cooler and heavier than surrounding air and will flow down slopes and collect in low areas. Also, air near the surface in city parks will be cooler than surrounding concrete and asphalt in urban areas, and this cool air can be carried by the wind short distances into adjacent hot areas of the city.

EFFECTS OF LANDSCAPE ELEMENTS

1. Deciduous woody plant: (a) provides shade in summer and allows solar radiation through in winter, and (b) has minimal effect on wind (see figure 5.1a).
2. Coniferous woody plant: (a) provides shade year-round, which is a benefit in summer, but a detriment in winter; and (b) can have a substantial effect on wind (see figure 5.1b).
3. Trellis: (a) if oriented toward the south, can provide shade in summer and allow solar radiation to pass through in winter (see figures 5.2a and 5.2b); (b) can provide a structure for deciduous

Figure 5.1 (a) Deciduous trees provide shade in summer when they are in leaf but allow a lot of solar radiation to pass through when they are leafless in winter. However, they have little effect on wind in winter.

Figure 5.1 (b) Coniferous trees provide shade in both summer and winter, but they will reduce wind flow in winter.

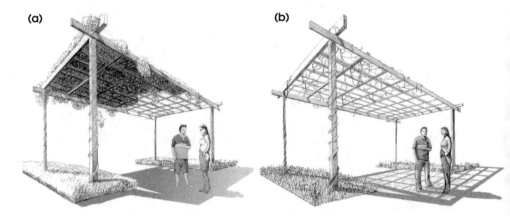

(a)

(b)

Figure 5.2 A trellis oriented to the south with a vine growing on it will (a) provide shade during the summer but (b) allow solar radiation to pass through in winter, improving the thermal comfort of people in both seasons.

vines to grow on, creating the same effect as deciduous trees; and (c) ineffective if oriented toward the east, north, or west.

4. Fence: (a) if oriented toward the east or west, can provide an area of shade in all seasons (largest in winter, smallest in summer) (see figures 5.3a and 5.3b); (b) not effective shade when oriented toward the north or south; (c) if oriented perpendicular to prevailing winter winds, can reduce winds in its lee; and (d) wind reduction zone will be largest if porosity of the fence is about 50 percent.

5. Surface: (a) light-colored materials will reflect solar radiation, having two effects: (1) the surface itself will stay cool, and (2) the reflected solar radiation will be available to be absorbed by other elements in the landscape; (b) dark-colored materials will absorb solar radiation, having two effects: (1) the surface will heat up and radiate terrestrial radiation, and (2) there will be very little solar radiation available to be absorbed by other elements in the landscape.

6. Overhanging roof: (a) when south facing, will provide shade in summer when the sun is high in the sky and will allow solar radiation to penetrate in winter when the sun is lower in the sky; (b)

(a)

(b)

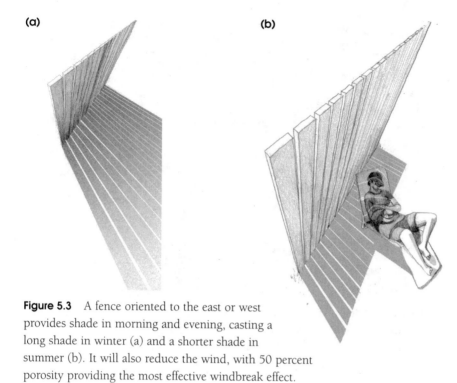

Figure 5.3 A fence oriented to the east or west provides shade in morning and evening, casting a long shade in winter (a) and a shorter shade in summer (b). It will also reduce the wind, with 50 percent porosity providing the most effective windbreak effect.

ineffective in modifying solar radiation in east-, west-, or north-facing orientations; and (c) has little effect on wind.

7. Water: (a) flat surface to the south can reflect solar radiation into a space; (b) has virtually no effect on wind; (c) can affect air temperature and air humidity if in a very enclosed space where air exchange is very small; and (d) when sprayed on a surface, can cool the surface, thus reducing the amount of terrestrial radiation emitted by that surface.

8. Topography: (a) south-facing slopes will receive the highest intensity of solar radiation; and (b) north-facing slopes will receive the lowest intensity of solar radiation.

9 Wall: (a) when oriented east-west, will receive high-intensity radiation during midday, with the highest intensity in winter when the sun is lower in the sky, raising the temperature of the wall so it will

Figure 5.4 A stone wall can absorb large amounts of solar radiation, particularly if the color of the stone is quite dark. This energy is stored in the rock and emitted as terrestrial radiation, a welcome addition to a person's energy budget on a cool evening.

emit more terrestrial radiation (see figure 5.4); (b) when oriented north-south, will receive high-intensity radiation during morning (on east face) and afternoon (on west face) in all seasons, again raising the temperature of the wall so that it will emit more terrestrial radiation; and (c) when covered with deciduous vines, will remain cool, so it will emit less terrestrial radiation.

PROTOTYPES

1. For a south-facing side of a house that will be in use in all seasons: overhanging roof, trellis on which grows a deciduous vine; coniferous hedge of medium porosity to the west and oriented north to south; deciduous vine-covered wall that is wetted intermittently

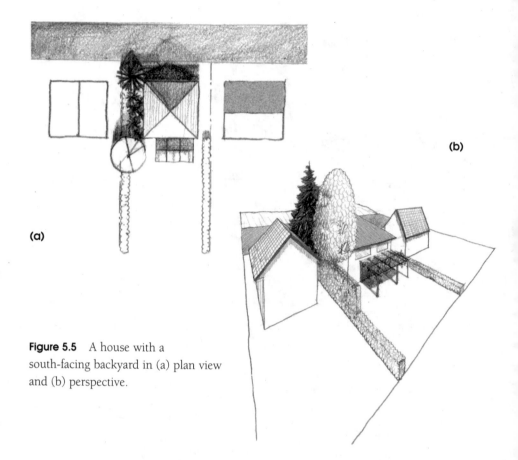

(b)

(a)

Figure 5.5 A house with a south-facing backyard in (a) plan view and (b) perspective.

by a fine mist of water; dark-colored surfaces to the south of the space; light-colored surfaces in the space; and vertical wall to the west (see figures 5.5a and 5.5b).

2. For a west-facing side of a house that will be in use in all seasons (with prevailing winds from the west to northwest): tall coniferous hedge or vine-covered vertical wall immediately on the west and northwest sides of the space; deciduous tree(s) to the southwest and west; deciduous vine-covered west-facing wall that is wetted intermittently by a fine mist of water; light-colored surfaces; and overhanging roof (see figures 5.6a and 5.6b).

(a)

(b)

Figure 5.6 A house with a west-facing backyard in (a) plan view and (b) perspective.

3. For an east-facing side of a house that will be in use in all seasons: no trees to the east or southeast; and no walls or vertical surfaces to obstruct solar access (see figures 5.7a and 5.7b).

4. For a north-facing side of a house that will be in use in all seasons (with prevailing winds from the west and northwest): tall coniferous hedge immediately to the west and northwest; light-colored vertical walls to the north, east, and west of the area to reflect solar radiation in; dark-colored surfaces in the area; overhead trellis covered with deciduous vines; and overhanging roof (see figures 5.8a and 5.8b).

QUICK REFERENCE

I've attempted to pull all the key information into one series of tables (see tables 5.1a–d). Determine the orientation of your site (the direction it is

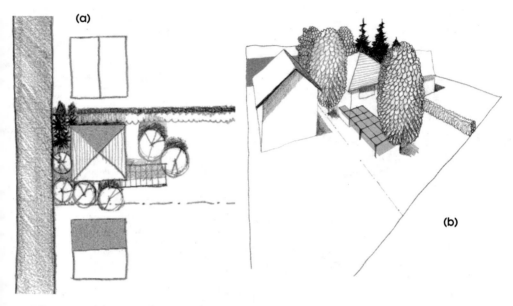

Figure 5.7 A house with an east-facing backyard in (a) plan view and (b) perspective.

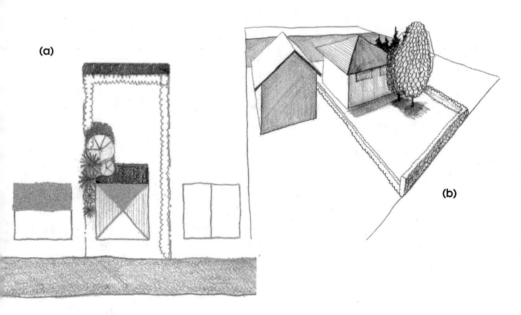

Figure 5.8 A house with a north-facing backyard in (a) plan view and (b) perspective

TABLE 5.1 (A, B, C, AND D) These tables provide a quick reference for deciding on appropriate design strategies based on the orientation of your site.

(A) South Facing

	Summer	Spring/fall	Winter
Typical Conditions	Sun: high at midday Wind: small effect on comfort	Sun: mid sky Wind: cooling	Sun: low at midday Wind: large effect on comfort
Time of Use	Morning and midday-day: passive use	Midday: passive or active use	Midday: passive or active use
Strategies	Sun: shade with overhead structure Wind: channel to increase speed	Sun: open Wind: windbreaks	Sun: open and vertical reflector Wind: windbreaks
Priorities	First: shield from sun Second: add wind Third: evaporative cooling	Equal priorities: shield from sun and reduce wind	First: reduce wind Second: provide sun Third: evaporative condensation

(B) West Facing

	Summer	Spring/fall	Winter
Typical Conditions	Sun: low in afternoon Wind: little effect on comfort	Sun: very low in afternoon Wind: cooling	Sun: none after midafternoon Wind: large effect on comfort
Time of Use	Morning: active or passive	Afternoon: active or passive	Afternoon: active
Strategies	Sun: vertical structure Wind: channel to increase speed	Sun: open access Wind: windbreaks to the west	Sun: open plus horizontal reflector Wind: windbreaks to the west
Priorities	First: shield from sun Second: avoid dark surfaces Third: evaporative cooling	Equal priorities: open to sun and reduce wind	First: reduce wind Second: provide access to sun

(C) North Facing

	Summer	Spring/fall	Winter
Typical Conditions	Sun: none Wind: cooling	Sun: none Wind: cooling	Sun: none Wind: large effect on comfort
Time of Use	Midday: active	Midday: very active	Midday: very active
Strategies	Sun: open access Wind: channel to increase	Sun: vertical reflector Wind: windbreaks on west side	Sun: vertical reflector Wind: windbreaks on west side
Priorities	First: channel wind to increase Second: evaporative cooling	First: reduce wind Second: reflect sun into space	First: reduce wind Second: reflect sun into space

(D) East Facing

	Summer	Spring/fall	Winter
Typical Conditions	Sun: low in morning Wind: moderate effect on comfort	Sun: very low in morning Wind: cooling	Sun: none before midmorning Wind: large effect on comfort
Time of Use	All day: Passive or active	Morning to midday: Passive or active	Midmorning to noon: active
Strategies	Sun: open access Wind: open access	Sun: open access Wind: windbreaks on north side	Sun: vertical reflectors Wind: windbreaks on north side
Priorities	First: allow sun access until midmorning Second: evaporative cooling	First: open access to sun Second: slow winds from north	First: slow winds from north Second: open access to sun

facing), and select the appropriate chart. For example, if you have a site or a location on your site that is facing to the south, you would select table 5.1a. The first row identifies typical conditions. These won't hold in all locations, so you will want to confirm them with your local climatic conditions, but they will represent many locations. For example, in summer the sun is high in the sky, and in winter it is low. If you have a site very near the equator, this will be less accurate, but for many mid- to high-latitude sites, this information will be correct. The wind will likely have little effect on people's comfort as the air temperature will likely be quite high. The next section suggests the most microclimatically appropriate time of use and level of activity for this space. In summer, this is an ideal location for passive activities around midday. It would be an ideal location for an outdoor café or a plaza where office workers might want to get outside and eat their lunch. In winter, it is also a midday place but people will likely have to be doing something active to generate internal energy to stay comfortably warm.

The next section gives suggestions for modifying the sun and the wind in summer and winter, and a suggestion for how to do this. For example, for summertime use, you should reduce the sun shining into this space; a solid overhead structure would be most effective for this.

A later section lists the most important design interventions in priority order. For the south in summer, the first priority is to provide shade, the second is to allow the wind to pass through, and the third would be to provide wet surfaces so that evaporative cooling can take place, which will reduce the temperatures of surfaces and reduce the terrestrial radiation emitted.

Once you have used this figure to determine which elements of the microclimate you should be modifying, use figure 5.9 to identify ways that your goals can be achieved. This figure is set up so that each of the different microclimate elements are listed down the left side of the page and different strategies for modifying them are listed across the page. Ways that you can make an outdoor space *feel cooler* to people are on the left, and as you move across the page to the right, the strategies transition to things

Make it *feel* cooler ← ─────────────── → Make it *feel* warmer

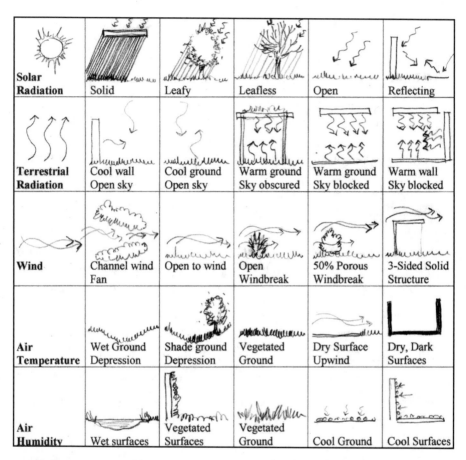

Solar Radiation	Solid	Leafy	Leafless	Open	Reflecting
Terrestrial Radiation	Cool wall Open sky	Cool ground Open sky	Warm ground Sky obscured	Warm ground Sky blocked	Warm wall Sky blocked
Wind	Channel wind Fan	Open to wind	Open Windbreak	50% Porous Windbreak	3-Sided Solid Structure
Air Temperature	Wet Ground Depression	Shade ground Depression	Vegetated Ground	Dry Surface Upwind	Dry, Dark Surfaces
Air Humidity	Wet surfaces	Vegetated Surfaces	Vegetated Ground	Cool Ground	Cool Surfaces

Figure 5.9 Use this diagram to help in deciding how the microclimates on your site can be modified. The figure is set up so that each of the different microclimate elements is listed down the left side of the page, and different strategies for modifying them are listed across the page. Ways that you can make an outdoor space *feel cooler* to people are on the left, and as you move across the page to the right the strategies transition to things that make an outdoor space *feel warmer*. Also, in general, the actions at the top of the chart are more effective than those nearer the bottom of the chart.

that make an outdoor space *feel warmer*. Also, in general, the actions at the top of the chart are more effective than those nearer the bottom of the chart.

ACTION

So there you have it. You have the basic knowledge, skills, and values, plus a process that will allow you to design microclimatically appropriate places. *You* now know, but how can you convince others that microclimate needs to be a consideration? I introduced the idea of applied evolutionary psychology in an earlier section, and now I'd like to give you some more insight that will allow you to communicate your message in a way that will encourage others to listen, hear, and act accordingly. (All referenced works appear in the "Recommended Reading" section at the back of this book.) I will be making some broad generalizations that won't relate to everyone, but they will relate to many people, maybe even most people.

The first thing to remember is that people want to have control—especially of decisions that will affect their living environment. Baumeister (2005) suggests that people have a deeply rooted motivation to have an impact on their surroundings—their personal habitat.[1] He says that through *primary* control people try to change their environment to fit themselves, and through *secondary* control they are willing to change themselves to fit their environment. This willingness to change can sometimes be initiated through *interpretive* control, in which people are more willing to accept something if they understand the reason for it. People also apparently have *motivational plasticity*. This means that their motivations aren't set in stone and can actually change over time—again, possibly because of seeing things from a different perspective.

If you stop and think about this for a minute, it really begins to speak to the issue of communicating ideas to a client. First of all, the client has a deep-seated, subconscious desire to be in control not only of the process that is being followed but also of what the final environment is going to be.

So there is little value in *telling* them what they should do or how they should do it. However, there is a subconscious willingness on the client's part to accept new information and ideas *if they understand them*. So, a big part of your job is communicating ideas in a way that a client can understand. Some clues from evolutionary psychology can help you do this.

Ariely (2008) has taken many ideas from evolutionary psychology, tested them through brilliant and often amusing experiments, and applied them to behavioral economics. Several of these ideas can be applied to communicating with design clients, so let's consider a few of them and explore how they might be of value.

It's probably important that you first understand how people think and how they are likely to act and react to your ideas. People tend to be quite *systematic* and *predictable*—but are not necessarily rational. They will tend to make very quick decisions when first confronted with an issue or a question, and then they will typically use that as a basis for all future decisions about that topic. Ariely uses the analogy of a gosling imprinting on the first living being it sees when it comes out of the egg and for the rest of its life thinking that being is its parent. If a client has no previous experience with a topic, you have the opportunity to give them an appropriate starting point. If they already have an irrational opinion about a topic, you can attempt to update it by providing a new context and new way of looking at the topic.

People also tend to feel a *strong attachment* to what they have and tend to *focus on what they might lose*, rather than what they might gain, when making decisions. They will also probably see your suggestions from a different perspective than you intend them. For example, you might tell them about how wonderful it would be for them to have a sunny backyard, but they might be thinking of how hot that would be in midsummer or of how the drapes in the south-facing windows would fade.

Knowing these general human characteristics allows you to prepare for your first meeting. You have an opportunity to help a client develop an open-minded, positive attitude. One way to do this is to provide them with some positive literature about the kind of work your firm does, the positive outcomes you have had with clients, and the positive effects that the work has had on the natural environment. *(And you could give them a copy of this book!)* You can also strongly influence their attitude toward you by including testimonials from satisfied clients. People tend to be affected subconsciously by the opinions of others. They will also be influenced by a trend that they can join. If your specialization is going to be microclimatic design, it would be worthwhile showing clients several examples of previous projects that were very successful.

When you first meet face-to-face, it's important to give them a very positive first impression. This will become the basis for their future opinions of you. I was supporting a family while I was working on my PhD, and my solution to finding enough time for everything in my life was to get up quite early. I would start work by about 6:00 a.m. and, due to the fact that I was the only one in the lab for the first two or three hours, I was very efficient and got a lot of work done. I became known as an early riser, and that label has never gone away. You've heard the saying, "Establish yourself as an early riser and you can sleep in the rest of your life." Well, I know that it's true! And the same holds with establishing yourself as a bright, competent, reliable, creative (you fill in the additional adjectives) person the first time you meet a client.

It's important that your message is clear and easy to understand. Discuss one or two examples of situations similar to the client's where microclimate was *not* considered and the project was a failure. Follow this up with one or two examples where microclimate was considered and the project was successful. People need a context before they can decide if they want something or not. Positive and negative examples can provide this context.

Make sure that you keep your message simple. For example: *The design is going to create cool, pleasant places on hot summer days and sunny, warm places during the winter.* Invoke their imaginations so that they can *feel* how great the place is going to be. Be sure to give them three choices, and expect that they will select the middle option. You can further encourage them to select the most microclimatically appropriate choice by including what Ariely calls a *decoy*—a poor cousin of your brilliant solution.

People tend to want to keep their options open and will go to great lengths to make sure that an option is not closed off permanently. They will also tend to put off a decision as long as they can. Not everyone will act this way, but it is worth expecting that they will and being prepared to help them decide. When they waver, have some compelling information that supports your design and allow them the option of selecting some components of the rejected designs that you will fit into the final design.

THE LAST WORD

Microclimatic design has the potential to address many of the world's issues and problems. Climate change is beginning to affect living environments around the world. Energy is becoming more expensive. Lands are being lost to desertification. Populations continue to increase, which means more mouths to feed. Increases in wealth lead to expectations for a higher quality of life. All of these issues and many more have microclimate at their heart. This book has focused primarily on designing to create thermally comfortable outdoor environments for humans. The same principles can be applied, at different scales, to help resolve many other issues. Eventually, politicians and decision makers are going to be looking for solutions, real solutions, and when they do you'll be prepared.

APPENDIX

Think and Do Exercises

1. Imagine that you have to hatch a duck egg, where all you have is a heater and a fan. The egg has to be kept at about the temperature of your hand at all times. How do you make sure that the egg doesn't get too hot or too cool? The heater and the fan both have variable settings.

2. Imagine that a person who is lost and very cold calls you from their cell phone asking for advice on how to get warm and stay warm until the rescue team arrives. It is a cold, clear, windy winter day. Where would you direct the person in the landscape?

3. Think of a cool, clear, windy spring day when you have been asked to find the best place in the landscape to hold a wedding ceremony for your best friend. Where would you place the guests, and where would you position the bride and groom (and why)?

4. The wedding that you helped to plan has been postponed. It is now a hot, sunny summer day and you have been asked by your friend whether the place you selected for them the last time would still be the best place. What would you tell the friend?

5. Near noon on a sunny spring day, lie down on the north face of a hill and pretend that you are a low-growing shrub. Describe the solar radiation you feel. Now move on to the south face of the hill and describe the solar radiation you feel.

6. During a hot summer day, find a place where there is no protection from the sun, where there are light-colored surfaces that will reflect extra radi-

ation onto you, and where there is little or no wind. Describe how you feel—but don't stay there very long! Analyze the place to determine what site design decisions affected the microclimate and in what way.

For the think exercises, try drawing a diagram with arrows representing the flows of energy—one each for convective heat loss, evaporative heat loss, and so on. Make the thickness of the arrow proportional to the amount of energy. Identify the main flows of energy, and decide which ones you want to maintain and which you might want to reduce.

Notes

CHAPTER 1.   EXPERIENTIAL

1.   With apologies to those of you who are southern hemisphere dwellers, from this point on I am going to discuss everything from a "northern hemisphere" point of view. Those of you in the south will simply have to invert the information to make it apply to you. I figure that you have been doing this forever, while those in the north have seldom had to consider this point. While living for a few months in New Zealand, I bought a map that had south at the top of the page. It was so disorienting that I had to keep turning it upside down to read it.

2.   This is my guess at the number of generations that have passed since people emigrated out of Africa to populate the rest of the earth. There is a new generation about every twenty years, so over the past forty thousand years there have been about two thousand generations. Now that's a family reunion I'd love to attend!

CHAPTER 3.   COMPONENTS

1.   At a height of about a hundred kilometers (62 miles) above the earth, individual molecules will be kilometers apart. Each molecule has quite a bit of energy here, but very little is transferred from one molecule to another because they seldom meet.

2. Early French visitors mistook the lodgepole pine trees (*Pinus contorta latifolia*) for Jack pine (*Pinus banksiana*), which looks quite similar. The common name for this tree in French is *Cyprés*, and the misnomer stuck.

3. Well, almost the coldest weather. During the winter of 1819–1820, William Parry was searching for the elusive Northwest Passage around the top of Canada. He spent more than ten months frozen in the ice off Melville Island, and the cold was so intense at times that the mercury in the expedition's thermometers froze solid.

4. Despite Canada's officially mandating the use of the metric system more than a generation ago, certain measurements have never changed. Amount of rainfall is reported by climate stations in millimeters, but the general public knows the amounts only in inches. Similarly, the general public has never converted people's heights and weights, or oven temperatures, to metric.

5. Materials with high thermal admittances will readily allow heat to move into the material so the surface temperature doesn't change much as a result. Materials with low thermal admittance will not allow heat to move easily into and through them, so the energy collects at the surface and causes the surface temperature to rise. Surfaces with high thermal admittance will have only small temperature differences between day and night, while those with low values can have large diurnal temperature differences.

CHAPTER 4. MODIFICATION

1. There is no general agreement on the various scales of climate and the prefixes that describe them. It would be convenient if the scales related to the metric system, so I have devised a system that goes with the *rule of ten*. In this system, *micro*climates are all sizes up to 100 meters (328 feet) in dimension; *moso*climates are from 100 meters to 1,000 meters (328 feet to 3,281 feet), or 0.1 kilometer to 1 kilometer (.06 mile to 0.6 mile); *miso*climates are from 1 kilometer to 10 kilometers (0.6 mile to 6.2 miles); *meso*climates are from 10 kilometers to 100 kilometers (6.2 miles to 62 miles); and *macro*climates are larger than 100 kilometers.

2. There are many winter days in southern Ontario where it is very possible to sit outside and have a meal if the space has been microclimatically

designed. When high-pressure systems prevail and the temperature is below freezing, there is often clear sky, allowing a high intensity of solar radiation, and light winds that can easily be reduced further by strategically placed windbreaks. Design of surface materials, colors, orientation, and so forth can create a wonderfully comfortable outdoor space for a few hours even in the midst of winter.

RECOMMENDED READING

These books are listed in order from what I consider to be the easiest to read and understand to the most complex and in depth.

Hopper, Leonard J. 2007. *Landscape Architectural Graphic Standards*. Hoboken, NJ: Wiley. 1074 pages.
  Several sections in this book provide the basics of solar radiation, wind, climate, microclimate modification, and air quality in a form that can be used directly in design. There is a student version of the book as well, which is much smaller but retains the microclimate pieces.
Sullivan, Chip. 2002. *Garden and Climate*. New York: McGraw-Hill. 263 pages.
  This is a beautifully illustrated book that received a national award from the American Society of Landscape Architects. The illustrations are outstanding and the text very readable, and the book provides an experiential view of microclimate modification. There are many examples of historic precedent and vernacular design.
Brown, G. Z., and Mark DeKay. 2001. *Sun, Wind and Light: Architectural Design Strategies*. 2nd ed. New York: Wiley. 382 pages.
  This is a very well-illustrated and interesting book, but as the title suggests, it is more oriented toward architecture with relatively little about outdoor environments or human thermal comfort. However, it contains many valuable diagrams and explanations that will definitely enhance your understanding of microclimate.
Brown, Robert D., and Terry J. Gillespie. 1995. *Microclimatic Landscape Design: Creating Thermal Comfort and Energy Efficiency*. New York: Wiley. 193 pages.

If you want a bit more detail on any microclimatic design concepts, take a look at this book. The information is still current, but unfortunately the computer programs are out of date. Two recent papers have provided an updated version of the COMFA model: (1) N. A. Kenny, J. S. Warland, R. D. Brown, and T. J. Gillespie, Part A: Assessing the performance of the COMFA outdoor thermal comfort model on subjects performing physical activity, *International Journal of Biometeorology* 53(5) (2009): 415–28; and (2) N. A. Kenny, J. S. Warland, R. D. Brown, and T. J. Gillespie, Part B: Revisions to the COMFA outdoor thermal comfort model for application to subjects performing physical activity 53(5) (2009): 429–41.

Oke, T. R. 1987. *Boundary Layer Climates*. 2nd ed. New York: Routledge. 435 pages.

Originally published in 1978, this book has been a classic for more than three decades. In my opinion, this is the best book ever written on the science of microclimate. The theory is explained very clearly and effectively, but you have to make the connection with design yourself. If you want a more complete, in-depth understanding of microclimates, this book will provide it.

Campbell, Gaylon S., and John M. Norman. 1998. *An Introduction to Environmental Biophysics*. 2nd ed. New York: Springer. 286 pp.

If you read and understand Oke and want to go into even more depth, this is the book for you. It provides theoretical foundations and equations for almost all aspects of the microclimate.

There are also a couple of references on evolutionary psychology that I think are quite useful and interesting.

Ariely, D. 2008. *Predictably Irrational: The Hidden Forces That Shape Our Decisions*. New York: Harper Collins. 304 pages.

Baumeister, Roy F. 2005. *The Cultural Animal: Human Nature, Meaning, and Social Life*. New York: Oxford University Press. 450 pages.

Index

Note: Page numbers followed by "f" or "t" indicate figures or tables, respectively

Deciduous woody plants, 121, 147, 147f
Decision making, by clients, 132–33, 159
Decks, in British Columbia, 88–89
Decoys, in communication with clients, 161
Design
critical component design (CCD), 107–9
foundation of, for thermal comfort, 6
functions of microclimate in, 19–20
humidity modification through, 58
as institution in Japan, 30
See also Microclimatic design
Design options for clients, 133
Design process
climate in, 109–17
communication in, 110, 129–34, 138
energy budgets in, 122–23
evaluation in, 110, 134–35
microclimate consideration in, 43–44, 91, 100–102
microclimate modification in, 110, 122–29
microclimate objectives in, 134–35
performance objectives in, 123–24
precedents in, 110, 117
site assessment in, 110, 118–24
Design strategies
for east-facing site, 155
for north-facing site, 155
for south-facing site, 154
for west-facing site, 154
Design styles, in future of microclimate design, 104
Development projects, 133
Dew point, 89–90

Diffuse radiation, 68–69
Diurnal patterns in local winds, 119–20

E

Earth, 61–63
Earth's atmosphere, 61, 75–76
Eastern white cedar, 78
East-facing side of house, prototypes for, 152, 153f
East-facing site, design strategies for, 155
East-facing slopes, 104
Elizabeth II, Saskatchewan tour, 85
Enduring microclimate hypothesis, 13
End user considerations, 133
Energy budgets
concept application, 92
in the design process, 122–23
modeling, 7–11
parked cars and, 15–17, 93
of a person, 6–8, 10–11, 70–71
radiation and, 86–87
terrestrial radiation in, 87–88
Equatorial regions, 75, 103
Evaluation, in design process, 110, 134–35
Evaporation, 9–10, 57, 87–88, 90
Evolutionary psychology, 143, 158–59
Evolution of humans, 130–31
Experiments, 64–65, 163–64

F

Fahrenheit, Daniel, 49
Fans, 101
Fear, in humans, 131
Fences, 77–78, 78f, 148, 149f
First Nations University, 29, 30f